RYAN LIBRARY
IONA COLLEGE
NEW ROCHELLE, N. Y.

UNIVERSITY OF ILLINOIS

INSTITUTE OF LABOR AND

INDUSTRIAL RELATIONS

National Economic Planning by Collective Bargaining

THE FORMATION OF AUSTRIAN

WAGE, PRICE, AND TAX POLICY

AFTER WORLD WAR II

by

MURRAY EDELMAN

*Associate Professor of Political Science
and Labor and Industrial Relations*

38866

338.9436
E 21

Copyright 1954 by the University of Illinois
Manufactured in the United States of America
Library of Congress Catalogue Card No. 54-62960

Foreword

America's prominence in world politics carries with it many responsibilities, not the least of which is the duty to understand foreign political and economic institutions. It is probably not chance that the most penetrating studies of American government have been made by friendly foreign observers, and a nation that has benefited from the work of Bryce and DeTocqueville would be short-sighted indeed to fail to recognize the values of comparative scholarship that gives us a broad and sympathetic perspective from which to understand our own as well as other peoples' institutions.

Although this volume deals with a country that is no longer a major force in the councils of nations, it serves admirably to bring into sharp focus the social mechanics that lead all nations in times of emergency to do some central planning with respect to sharing of the national product among those who contribute to it. Austria chose to plan by negotiation among representatives of economic organizations. The United States has used this device occasionally in its wartime economic stabilization programs. For a rather different purpose, the State of Illinois has followed a similar process in amending its unemployment compensation, workmen's compensation, and mine safety laws. The Institute has published a study of the Illinois practice,[1] and members of its staff have prepared a critical analysis of the wartime experiment in tripartitism at the national level.[2] The present study adds perspective and meaning to these American experiences and, we hope, tells an interesting story in itself. Springfield, Illinois, Washington, D.C., and Vienna, Austria, can learn a great deal from each other, and students of labor and industrial relations can learn from all of them.

The author has been given full freedom and responsibility for making his findings and reaching conclusions.

ROBBEN W. FLEMING, *Director, Institute of Labor and Industrial Relations*

---

[1] Gilbert Y. Steiner, *Legislation by Collective Bargaining: The Agreed Bill in Illinois Unemployment Compensation Legislation* (Urbana: University of Illinois Institute of Labor and Industrial Relations, 1951).
[2] W. Ellison Chalmers, Milton Derber, and William H. McPherson (eds.), *Problems and Policies of Dispute Settlement and Wage Stabilization During World War II* (Washington: U.S. Department of Labor Bulletin No. 1009, 1950).

Acknowledgments

A real difficulty with empirical investigations is their inevitable imposition on the time and energies of busy men and women who have to be interviewed or asked for data. Being relatively modest in scope and based largely on documentary materials, the present study did not sin in this respect as grossly as some. But this was doubtless small consolation to the many individuals who did cheerfully talk to me and answer my demands for detail with patience and perception. So far as the Austrians involved were concerned, the experience brought gratifying reassurance that attempts at scholarship are regarded as worthy of encouragement and as irrelevant to the animosities and annoyances that go with suffering in war and prolonged occupation in peacetime.

Officials and staff members of the Austrian Trade Union Federation and of the Chambers of Labor, Trade, and Agriculture, both in Vienna and in the provinces, were unfailingly cooperative, helpful, and *gemütlich*. Irwin Tobin, American labor attaché in Vienna, provided a great deal of invaluable background information and advice and some useful introductions. Einar Edwards, MSA labor adviser in Austria, and Theodor Neumann, MSA economist, supplied some enlightening data not elsewhere available. Professors Milton Derber, Phillips Garman, Charles Hagan, William McPherson, and Richard Wilcock of the University of Illinois read the manuscript and criticized it with relish. The knowledge that Barbara Dennis was to edit the monograph made writing it a good deal easier.

Two other acknowledgments are more basic than any of these, in a sense: to the United States Government for a generous Fulbright grant; and to my wife, Bacia, for all kinds of help, including encouragement to spend a lot of time studying wage-price agreements when the temptation was great to spend more of it enjoying Austrian opera and Alps.

M.E.

Table of Contents

CHAPTER 1 The Problem and Its Setting

Since the end of the war, Austria has been a laboratory for a novel and instructive experiment in economic planning and labor-management negotiation. Wages, prices, pensions, and taxes have five times been renegotiated by collective bargaining among management, labor, and agricultural organizations as a method of apportioning the small national product among these competing economic groups. For anyone seeking to understand the relationships among political organizations, economic groups, and public policies, analysis of the operation of this Austrian device for coping with its economic dilemmas affords a clarifying perspective and a basis for reaching some important hypotheses about public policy formation in general.

It is particularly enlightening to contrast this arrangement with the American program of allocating such powers to separate governmental or private organizations for fixing wages, prices, pensions, and taxes. One of the difficulties in systematic description of social events is the identification of a political system for the management of human affairs. The Austrian system has the enormous advantage of making it possible to observe the positions of economic groups, the precise extent to which these groups are willing to compromise with rival positions, and, most important of all, the exact fashion in which this set of activities is translated into official public acts. For the student, this is a welcome difference from the more common American system in which activity is so widely dispersed that most models for description will not reveal clear answers.

ECONOMIC TRENDS, GOVERNMENTAL ORGANIZATION, AND PUBLIC POLICY

It has been aptly suggested that facts and data are never "given" but always "taken." Which data a student chooses to take and how he organizes them is a function of the definition of his subject and of his system of assumptions and hypotheses. Readers are entitled to know what this system is and to judge for themselves its limitations, its boldness, and its utility for the particular study.

The present study proceeds from two major hypotheses. The first of these is that changes in public policy affecting prices, wages, taxes, and pensions occur in some determinable relationship to economic trends. This proposition is examined in the study, and a relationship among the factors named is suggested. The hypothesis rests on certain assumptions and definitions which cannot and need not be tested because they make no allegation about "fact," but rather define the perspective from which the writer chose to view his data. These assumptions follow:

1. At any given point in time, various groups have differing estimates of the consequences of a proposed or extant public policy, and the difference is manifested in their behavior.

2. These groups do not conform exactly to the membership of any private or public organization. As conditions change, the composition of the groups and the intensity of their values change.

3. Public policy changes are the resultant of changes in the intensity of such group evaluations.

The second major hypothesis on which the study tries to throw light is that the nature of the organization to formulate public policy has a predictable bearing on the relative influence of the various groups concerned with the policy and therefore on policy change. The assumption here is that organization channels economic data and information on the special problems of various groups. It is hypothesized that alternative organizational forms and jurisdictions connote differences in the sensitivity of the unit to particular demands. The more exclusively an organizational unit is concerned and informed about the problems and needs of a particular group, the more influential that group is likely to be in policy formation. Organization may also fix the limits within which policy alternatives are possible, for higher organizational echelons or private organizations can sometimes veto, weaken, or abolish an organizational unit that strays in its policies from what is acceptable to the "constituent" unit.[1]

During the seven-year period under consideration, the Austrian economic scene experienced some major changes, and trends in production, employment, industrial prices, farm prices, wages, pensions, and taxes were often strikingly uneven. Occasionally an influence from outside the domestic economy caused one of them to spurt while others lagged. There is therefore ample opportunity to look for a relationship between trends and policy changes.

With respect to the significance of organizational factors in policy formation, several control devices permitting rough conclusions are available. When a policy was being debated, it was often possible to

---

[1] For an analysis of these propositions see Murray Edelman, "Governmental Organization and Public Policy," *Public Administration Review*, Autumn, 1952, pp. 276-283.

observe divergent points of view in organizations with different jurisdictions and at different points in the hierarchy. It is also possible
to compare the Austrian organizational set-up with the American
institutions for wartime price and wage control, although not very
precisely. Probably more rewarding than either of these is careful ob-
servation of the process within various organizational units in an effort
to see which considerations account for the ultimate position of the
organization.

The two approaches suggested here, that of economic trends and
that of governmental organization, are only conceptually different.
They involve study of much the same data from different perspectives.
They accordingly yield different but supplementary observations,
especially as to process and relations.

THE POLITICAL AND ECONOMIC SETTING

The five wage-price agreements were political compromises as well
as economic transactions and are therefore understandable only in the
context of Austrian political institutions. Postwar Austria is a federal
republic. Its population numbers 6,918,959 of whom 1,760,784 live in
Vienna.[2] Although the constitution reserves certain powers to the nine
provinces, the economic functions considered in this paper are exercised
by the central government. Except to the limited extent noted below,
the four occupying powers have not interfered in the formulation of
the wage-price agreements.[3]

The largest political parties are the People's Party, whose support
comes chiefly from farmers and business, and the Socialist Party,
which draws support in the main from labor. Since 1946 these two
parties have cooperated in a coalition government headed by a chancellor from the People's Party.[4] The chancellor and cabinet serve at
the pleasure of the lower house of Parliament, the National Council.

Since the war the People's Party has held a slim plurality of the
seats over the Socialists.[5] The Communists have controlled 4 to 5 per
cent of the seats, and since 1949 the League of Independents, a rightist
party with a strong following of former Nazis, has held 6 to 10 per

[2] Based on the census of June 1, 1951.
[3] The Allied Control Agreement of June 28, 1946, provides that any of the four powers may
veto a change in constitutional law, but the concurrence of all four is required to veto ordinary
legislation. The Soviet element has consistently opposed the agreements, but could not unilaterally
prevent their becoming effective.
[4] The one Communist member of the coalition cabinet withdrew voluntarily in December,
1947.
[5] In the three elections for representation in the National Council since the war, the number of seats won by the various parties was as follows:

	1945	1949	1953
People's Party	85	77	74
Socialists	76	67	73
League of Independents	..	16	14
Communist and Left Bloc	4	5	4

cent. Cabinet posts have been divided between the two coalition parties. The Ministries directly concerned with the subjects covered in the wage-price agreements are Social Affairs, Interior, Trade, Agriculture and Forestry, and Finance. Socialists have headed the first two and People's Party members the last three.

In postwar Austria other organizations, more directly representative of specific economic interests, have supplemented and even supplanted these governmental bodies to a remarkable degree in the formulation of economic policy.

THE CHAMBERS

Historically, management, labor, and agricultural groups in Austria have been accustomed to turn to government for favors to a far greater extent than has been the case in America. The Austrian federal and provincial governments have long recognized and encouraged these economic groups to organize for the explicit purpose of advising on and influencing public policy. In the case of labor, there is thus not only a Trade Union Federation, whose main task it is to negotiate with — and on occasion fight — management, but also Chambers[6] of Labor in each province, legally charged with the function of representing the interests of workers in the enactment of labor laws and in their administration. Chambers of Trade and Chambers of Agriculture similarly act for these sectors of the economy. These three Chambers, together with the Trade Union Federation, were the key negotiators of the wage-price agreements. They are in some ways strange institutions to Americans and warrant brief description if their roles in the formulation of the agreements is to be understood.

Membership and dues are compulsory. The federal law establishing the Chambers of Trade defines as members "all physical and legal persons" authorized to operate an independent enterprise in commerce (foreign or domestic), industry, finance, credit, or insurance. Similarly, all wage and salary earners must pay dues to the Chamber of Labor although they are not called "members." The Chambers of Agriculture are established by provincial laws with similar provisions.

Each type of enterprise listed above as members of the Chamber of Trade constitutes a "section" in each of the nine provincial Chambers,[7] and the federal Chamber is divided into similar sections. Each section elects a chairman and meets in periodic assemblies. There are also assemblies of the provincial Chambers and of the federal Chamber, each electing a president, praesidium, executive council, and working com-

---

[6] The plural form is used here because there is a separate Chamber in each province. When the singular form appears later, it denotes the provincial Chambers acting together or a representative of all of them.

[7] I.e., foreign commerce, domestic commerce, industry, finance, credit, and insurance.

mittees. The federal praesidium consists of the president of the federal Chamber and two vice-presidents. Rank and file members vote only for the lowest echelon of officers. Federal and provincial officials are thus elected indirectly by delegates to their respective assemblies.

The Chambers of Labor differ from this pattern in several important respects. There is no federal Chamber, but the Chamber for the Province of Vienna represents the others in contacts with the federal government, and the president of the Vienna Chamber presides at occasional meetings of an assembly representing all the provinces. Each provincial Chamber is divided into sections representing wage earners, salary earners, and public employees, respectively, and "members" of the Chamber consist of delegates elected by workers in each of these categories, voting separately.[8] Members serve five-year terms and elect a president, two vice-presidents, and an executive committee with the same tenure. One-half of 1 per cent of every worker's salary is checked off to support the Chamber.

As each provincial Chamber of Agriculture operates on the basis of a different statute, there is no uniformity as to organization. In general, however, choice of top officers is indirect, and in some provinces, members[9] do not vote at all. The presidents of the eight Chambers[10] meet from time to time to discuss matters of common interest, although there is no legal provision for this practice. The Chamber for Lower Austria normally carries on necessary contacts with federal government agencies on behalf of the others.

The chief functions of all three Chambers are quite similar so far as public policy is concerned. Though the laws establishing them list a great many purposes, they add up to (1) giving reports, advice, and recommendations to public legislative and administrative bodies on appropriate matters; (2) performing all tasks which are in the common economic welfare of their members; (3) maintaining special surveillance over the government departments most directly concerned with their economic welfare; (4) participating directly and formally in the work of a large number of special government boards charged with regulating specific economic problems, including foreign trade, investment policy, control of scarce raw materials, price and wage control, housing, and others; (5) compiling statistical data and undertaking such statistical and other studies as are necessary to carry out these functions. The federal Chamber of Trade and each of the provincial Chambers of Trade also bargain collectively with unions. The

---

[8] Each voter must have worked for at least one year. Provincial Chambers consist of at least 48 members and not more than 144, the number varying according to the number of constituents entitled to vote.

[9] All persons engaged in farming are "members."

[10] There is none for Vienna.

Chambers of Labor prepare materials to aid in bargaining sessions, but leave actual negotiation to the unions.

The Chamber of Trade has long exercised tight controls over prices, and the various industrial sections of the Chamber have strongly influenced local licensing authorities in the grant or denial of permission to establish new businesses.[11] Conventions which meet annually or more often serve as forums in which the leadership reports to the rank and file on leading problems and seeks to win support for its policies. To a substantially lesser extent the representatives of the membership utilize these conventions to report rank and file opinion to the leadership.

Finally, there is a substantial overlap of leadership among the Chambers, the political parties, and governmental legislative and executive organs. The present chancellor of Austria was formerly president of the federal Chamber of Trade and chairman of the People's Party Caucus in Parliament. His predecessor as chancellor was a leading figure in the Chambers of Agriculture. The Minister of Social Affairs, a leading Socialist, is also president of Austria's largest union, the Metal Workers, and of course extremely influential in the Chamber of Labor. The president of the Trade Union Federation is also vice-speaker of the lower house of Parliament and chairman of the Socialist Caucus there.

The Austrian Trade Union Federation was also a party to the wage-price negotiations, perhaps to "balance" the agriculture-business groups with two labor organizations, although this is nowhere explicitly stated. About 67 per cent of Austria's wage and salary workers or almost a fifth of the nation's total population belong to the Trade Union Federation. The Federation is composed of 16 unions.

ADVERSARY INTERESTS WITHIN THE PRIVATE ORGANIZATIONS

Reliance on organizations supposedly based upon common economic objectives for a major role in public economic policy formulation did not mean that the members of any one of these organizations really had common aims in all economic policies. Scrutiny of the activities of the membership of these bodies and of the positions taken by factions within them on some key issues demonstrates, on the contrary, that there was a great deal of potential discord within each of them; and that when a consensus was achieved, it was a function of compromise in the light of the particular set of economic circumstances that prevailed at the time. That this point may stand out more clearly in the chronology of events that follows, it will be useful to mention

---

[11] Cf. Harry Johnstone, *The Restraint of Competition in the Austrian Economy* (Vienna: Office of the U. S. High Commissioner, 1951).

some of the leading internal differences in interest within the Chambers, the political parties, and the Trade Union Federation. This does not, of course, comprise an exhaustive list, but only some significant illustrations.

In the Chamber of Trade, manufacturers of consumer goods for the domestic market were constantly concerned that there be adequate consumer purchasing power, especially in the immediate postwar period when wages and living costs were extremely low. Makers of commodities for export and exporters themselves were inevitably far less sensitive to domestic wage demands and, indeed, gained better exchange terms if production costs were kept as low as possible. On the issues of credit restrictions and monetary reform, banking groups in the Chamber were far more adamantly opposed to governmental controls than their colleagues.

Within the People's Party an even wider range of potential and actual internal discord was evident. The Party was divided into business, farmer, and labor sections, and differences in objectives as well as in emphasis frequently appeared. The labor section was almost wholly representative of white collar workers and had relatively little influence, but it often took public positions quite different from those expounded by the other sections. Farm press organs sometimes sniped at industrial price increases, though care was usually taken to resolve industry-agriculture differences before wage-price negotiations began.

Dairy and grain producers often sought divergent policy emphases within the Chambers of Agriculture to solve their respective problems. No overt conflict appeared, however, for their objectives were not incompatible.

Several types of conflict appeared within the Trade Union Federation. The general secretary of the Federation's Executive Committee in the province of Salzburg complained to the writer that Federation leaders in Vienna did not always understand the needs of Salzburg workers, especially those arising from the fact that prices were higher in Salzburg than in Vienna.[12] Similar views were probably held by union officials in other outlying provinces.

More important were differences in party allegiance on the part of Federation members. On the basis of the 1952 Works Council elections and statements by various Federation officials, the following estimates as to relative party strength in the Federation through most of this period are probably not far from accurate:

SOCIALIST	73 PER CENT
COMMUNIST	12 PER CENT
PEOPLE'S PARTY	10 PER CENT
LEAGUE OF INDEPENDENTS	5 PER CENT

[12] Salzburg was the headquarters of the American occupation forces in Austria.

On the "bread and butter" trade union issues, these party affiliations made little difference. Federation negotiators could usually count on full rank and file support on wage demands even when the People's Party was taking a dim view of any increases. Rank and file rejection of the Communist line of much higher wage demands could not as easily be assumed, and the Communist position exerted a real upward thrust both on Federation wage demands and on final settlements. Party allegiance did make a difference on long-range economic and policy planning, especially nationalization policy, and on such measures the Socialist officers of the Federation could be assumed to be speaking only for the Socialist rank and file.

The observations about interest differences within the Trade Union Federation apply fairly aptly to the Chambers of Labor as well, for the composition of the two organizations was largely the same — the chief difference between them being one of function. Because the Chamber represented all workers, including the unorganized, differences based upon pay level and strength of union organization were more apparent in it than in the Federation. Vacillations by the two organizations on the issue of entering into general agreements rather than individual negotiations by the separate unions represented to a considerable degree a conflict between the demands of the poorly organized and unorganized on the one hand and the optimum interests of the strongly organized on the other. More specifically, the urge to equalize the wage structure so as to assure the lowest wage earners a subsistence living standard clashed with the desires of skilled and white collar labor in increasing measure as production and productivity improved.

Like any political party, the Socialists faced not only the task of satisfying factions of its membership but of attracting wider support among non-members. So far as the first of these problems is concerned, the following breakdown of party membership by occupation is instructive:[13]

WAGE EARNERS	40 PER CENT
SALARIED PERSONNEL	25 PER CENT
HOUSEWIVES	20 PER CENT
SELF-EMPLOYED	10 PER CENT
PENSIONERS	5 PER CENT

Like the labor organizations, then, the Party contained built-in factions based upon wage level and skill of occupation. The pensioner group, into which most members of the others could expect one day to graduate, exerted a strong influence, especially as many non-member pensioners also had votes. Within each of the groups listed above were

---

[13] *Arbeiter-Zeitung*, March 31, 1951, p. 1.

intellectuals, relatively less concerned with the drives of their occupational groups than with Socialist doctrine. These exert a strong influence in any social democratic party, though they were clearly less significant in the postwar Austrian Socialist Party than they had been before 1934, when Otto Bauer, Julius Deutsch, and other intellectuals had exercised unchallenged leadership through sheer brilliance, parliamentary eloquence, and unexampled wit and zeal.[14]

Clearly, therefore, a statement by a leader of one of these organizations or by a sample of rank and file members at any time would have meaning for that moment and for the particular group which the respondent represented, but not necessarily any wider or continuing meaning. The support of any of these organizations for a particular economic policy must be defined by a specific statement of time and relevant circumstances and conditions. In what follows this volume undertakes that task of definition.

EARLY GROPINGS FOR A WAGE-PRICE ORGANIZATION AND POLICY, 1945-1947

Both in terms of governmental organization and in terms of a knowledge of what the situation required, it was inevitable that the first postwar years should produce makeshift solutions, often ineffective and requiring drastic revision. That inflation was a serious danger and that government controls would be needed were obvious. Seven years of Nazism and war had gutted the economy and seriously impaired its recuperative powers. The Nazis had linked the Austrian economy to the German war plant, cutting agricultural production, boosting the output of heavy industry, chemicals, oil, and hydroelectric power, and carelessly exploiting the resources of wood, ores, and oil, with no thought of the suitability of these measures for an independent, peacetime Austria or an integrated economy. The war had brought drastic shortages of capital and consumer goods, and bad weather in the first postwar years further injured agriculture and cut fuel supplies and power output to critical levels. Productivity was miserably low due to damaged and outmoded factories, severe malnutrition, poor training among the workers, and raw material shortages. The division of Austria into four occupation zones hampered internal trade, the more so as most heavy industries were situated in the western zones and most finishing industries and agriculture in the Soviet zone. In 1946, the national product was half of its prewar level.[15]

An inflationary complement to this picture of a reduced and dis-

---

[14] Cf. Charles Gulick, *Austria From Habsburg to Hitler* (Berkeley: University of California, 1948); G. E. R. Gedye, *Betrayal in Central Europe* (New York and London: Harper, 1939).
[15] Cf. Irving B. Kravis, "Prices and Wages in the Austrian Economy, 1938-47," *Monthly Labor Review*, January, 1948, pp. 20-27.

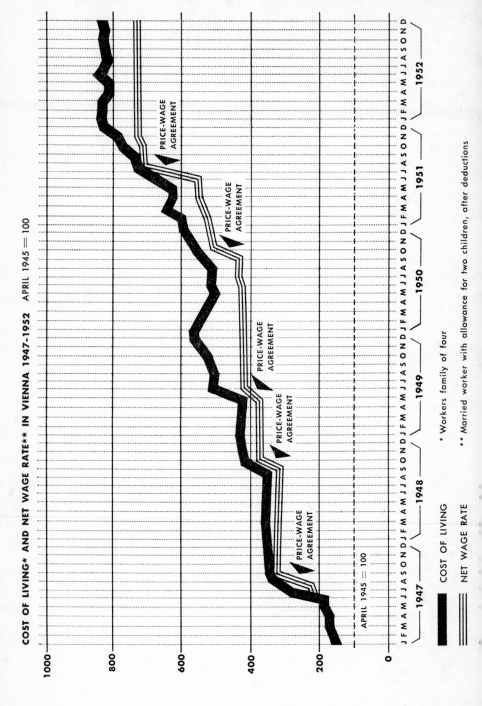

COST OF LIVING* AND NET WAGE RATE** IN VIENNA 1947-1952   APRIL 1945 = 100

* Workers family of four

** Married worker with allowance for two children, after deductions

COST OF LIVING

NET WAGE RATE

torted national product was an excessive supply of circulating currency. After VE-Day, German reichsmarks continued to pour into Austria from all parts of the shattered "Thousand-Year Empire." Although they had already lost their value in the countries of issuance, they were still legal tender in Austria. A currency conversion law of November 30, 1945, required the exchange of all marks for schillings, permitted the withdrawal from bank accounts of 150 schillings per head, and blocked the remainder in accounts available to the owner for only restricted use. Apart from the fact that it favored property owners, this proved a highly temporary improvement, for withdrawals from the blocked accounts and payments of bank notes to the occupying powers replenished the supply of currency, which reached its former level before the end of 1946.

A related and very potent inflationary factor was the gross disparity between Austrian and foreign prices at the end of the war. During the Nazi period wage and price ceilings and agricultural subsidies had kept food prices down, although somewhat more leeway had been permitted in the war production industries. The exposure of this hermetically sealed economy to world market prices, which had gone up three to five times since 1938, entailed a complicated and dangerous readjustment of the domestic wage-price structure.[16]

During the first two postwar years this readjustment was treated as if it involved separable price, wage, subsidy, and fiscal problems, for these questions were assigned to different governmental organizations for disposition. Not until events proved that the welfare of all economic sectors was seriously endangered by this arrangement was a different governmental pattern — the wage-price agreement — attempted late in 1947.

Immediately after liberation the several Allied military authorities determined the principles of price policy, with little coordination among the zones. All individual price increases needed the approval of an occupying power. With the law of July 17, 1945,[17] control over all prices, but not wages or salaries, was assigned to the Austrian government, although the Allies maintained some review authority.

A highly decentralized administrative pattern, according maximum influence to the various business groups seeking price increases,[18] was instituted. The Interior Ministry was given over-all responsibility, but the Ministry under whose jurisdiction the applicant for a price increase fell (Agriculture, Trade, et cetera) first negotiated directly with the applicant and then made recommendations to the Interior

---

[16] Cf. article by Ludwig Kostroun in the *Arbeiter-Zeitung*, July 22, 1947.
[17] BGBl 89/1945.
[18] Kravis, *op. cit.*

Ministry. Moreover, authority to make price decisions of minor or local significance was assigned to the executive magistrates of the Austrian provinces and districts. The Chambers were to advise the various Ministries on price questions. The Interior Ministry performed its functions under this law with a small staff and under great difficulties. Major applications were often brought by the Ministry concerned before an *ad hoc* council of Ministers, further reducing the ability of the Interior Ministry to hold the line or maintain over-all surveillance.

Until January, 1946, wages were controlled by an Inter-Allied Wage Board. Thereafter, the pattern of assigning control powers to the governmental agency subject to the greatest influence by the groups to be controlled was adopted, and regulation of wages was lodged in the Ministry of Social Affairs. A law of January 28, 1946,[19] created in the Ministry a Central Wage Commission consisting of two representatives of labor, two of management, and a deputy of the Minister of Social Affairs as chairman.[20] The Inter-Allied Control Board maintained authority to review wage decisions, but did very little after June, 1946.

As the present study is concerned primarily with a later period, a detailed account of wage and price movements during the first two years after liberation will not be presented here.[21] Suffice it to say that the official cost of living index rose from 105.0 in April, 1945 (April, 1938 = 100), to 177.7 in April, 1947, and to 275.8 in July, 1947 (after a more realistic method of measuring clothing prices was introduced), despite the announcement of stringent "principles" for the granting of price increases. The discontinuance of the German food subsidies unquestionably contributed to this upward surge. This index is a measure only of controlled, official prices. In point of fact, black market prices many times the legal amounts had to be paid to obtain a great many commodities. Wage increases during this period kept pace with official prices, a result sought by Central Wage Commission policy. Real wages declined because of the black market. The Austrian Institute of Economic Research said of Wage Commission operations, "The task of the Central Wage Commission was especially difficult because many labor demands met with feeble resistance from employers if they could pass on their increased wage costs in higher prices."

---

[19] BGBl 50/1946.

[20] For the information regarding governmental control organization in this early period I am indebted principally to the following: Josef Staribacher, "Ziele und Möglichkeiten der behördlichen Preisbildung und die Preisbildung in Österreich seit 1945" (Ph.D. dissertation, Vienna 1950), pp. 1-17; *Arbeiterkammer Jahrbuch*, 1946, pp. 124-125, and 1947, pp. 368-369; Kravis, *op. cit.*, pp. 24-27.

[21] For a competent account of this development and useful tables see Kravis, *op. cit.* Statistical tables that report living costs and earnings for this period as well as for subsequent years may be found in the Appendix of this volume, pp. 70-73.

The Commission did succeed, however, in preventing exorbitant variations in wage increases among different sectors of the working population and actually reduced prior differentials.[22]

A control device less likely to curb inflation would have been difficult to devise. Not only were the various control agencies subject to great pressure from groups seeking price and wage increases and to relatively little influence from anyone desiring to hold the line, but no responsible administrative body was in a position to see or do anything about the inflationary effects of the price rises on wages, of wages on prices, or even of the various prices on each other, except under great difficulties. A careful student of this program, Staribacher, says on this point, "Although only an independent agency would have been able to view the price questions from the point of view of their over-all economic effects, the Austrian arrangement made price control subject to a far-reaching extent to the influence of special interests."[23]

ORIGINS OF THE FIVE WAGE-PRICE AGREEMENTS

In an important sense, the origins of the five wage-price agreements have already been described. There was a strong inflationary potential and clear evidence that government agencies subjected to the unopposed influence of groups seeking higher prices or wages could not combat the inflationary trend. In these circumstances the only effective solution could have been the formulation of over-all wage-price-budgetary policy by a single organization within which rival groups would moderate each others' demands. It remains to be seen, however, how this organization came to be established when it did, how it came to revise its policies from time to time, and how it assumed its somewhat unusual form.

These questions can be answered most adequately through an analysis of the adversary and complimentary groups in their impact on various public policies in postwar Austria. Both on a priori grounds and from the speeches and writings of the time, it is obvious that immediately after the war all economic sectors and all political groups seeking to win their support had some very strong objectives in common: (1) reconstruction and improvement of productive facilities; (2) securing foreign economic aid for this purpose and also maintenance of at least a subsistence standard of living for the entire Austrian population; (3) the prevention of runaway inflation; (4) minimal support for those in greatest economic need, including, at various periods, pensioners, the lowest-paid wage earners, and farmers.

---

[22] Institut für Wirtschaftsforschung, *Monatsbericht*, April, 1947, p. 11.
[23] Staribacher, *op. cit.*, p. 10.

Although not all economic groups could be equally aware of the pressing importance of each of these policies, the organizations already described served to spread these common aims: to make labor alert, for example, to the bearing of plant improvement on jobs and wages and to make business aware of the inability of pensioners to support themselves without further help. The close ties of the economic Chambers to political parties seeking votes on a broad base and the constant discussions between the two coalition parties in the cabinet and at lower levels particularly promoted this phenomenon.

CHAPTER 2 The First Wage-Price Agreement

ECONOMIC DEVELOPMENTS PRIOR TO THE FIRST AGREEMENT

Statistical indexes of price and wage developments in an economy as disorganized as was the Austrian immediately after the war inevitably measure the boldness of the statisticians more accurately than the items purportedly computed. The available measures nevertheless serve our purposes roughly. The most useful Austrian cost of living index, that published by the Institute of Economic Research, tries to measure the living costs of a working class family of four persons in Vienna. Its most serious disadvantage is that it refers only to controlled prices and has not taken account of black market prices, even in the first postwar years when many goods simply were not available at the official prices. This defect is partially remedied by a supplementary table showing the ratio of black market to official prices. The Institute warns, however, that the index is an extremely rough instrument, particularly when used to compare relative increases in earnings and living costs. The latter are likely to be understated, and both indexes are slow in reflecting changes. In spite of these reservations, the following conclusions about price-wage developments prior to the first wage-price agreement seem warranted.[1]

Because of the dire predicament of the lowest paid workers, the wages of unskilled labor and of female labor were permitted by the Central Wage Commission to increase faster than those of the higher-paid workers. For a year after April, 1945, wage controls were fairly stringent. Living costs and wages rose relatively little and together. Starting in the spring of 1946 there was a definite relaxing in controls, with the tempo of increases quite sharply accelerated. Reviewing economic developments of the year 1946, the Institute of Economic Research declared that in the last months of that year wages and prices took on the character of a spiral, with no particular wage or price structure discernible. In May, 1947, a significant new wave of price increases occurred, including for the first time the costs of processing raw materials. A downward trend in black market prices

---

[1] The data on wage and price developments are based upon the *Monthly Reports* of the Austrian Institute of Economic Research and the *Yearbooks* of the Austrian Chamber of Labor.

remained fairly consistent during these years, due very likely to the importation of UNRRA supplies and the curtailment of effective demand as low wage workers exhausted their savings.

Postwar wage levels were miserably low. As late as October, 1946, the Austrian Institute of Economic Research reported that the lowest wages barely covered half the physiological subsistence minimum.[2] As nearly as can be ascertained, wage increases from April, 1945, to October, 1947, approximately kept pace with the increase in official prices, although there was much seesawing, the picture varied as to industry, and the generalization applies only to averages.

Although agricultural prices were more generally and more tightly controlled than industrial prices, the pattern of decentralized government regulation made it possible for farmers, as well as businessmen and wage earners, to secure gains. The tactics of agricultural groups early in 1946 illustrate the point. Desperate food shortages in the cities, and especially in Vienna, immediately after the fighting stopped had led to the establishment of quotas of various farm products which the farmers were supposedly obligated to ship to the urban areas. These quotas were frequently not met, and in the first months of 1946 shipments of slaughter cattle to Vienna reached a low point. To remedy this agricultural leaders asked that farmers be awarded premium payments to induce them to meet their quotas. For this purpose the Ministry of Agriculture made available a support of 100 schillings for every 100 kilograms of live weight. This created a *fait accompli* for future price determinations, for nobody could consider fixing the minimum price at a point under the older price increased by the premium. The premium payments also necessitated a later increase in vegetable prices to protect price relationships.

It is clear that for more than two years price and wage adjustments were made through the initiative of business and labor groups and through collective bargaining negotiations, and that these adjustments were approved quite freely by the wage and price control authorities, acting separately.

Although continuation of the inflationary spiral probably would have led eventually to closer coordination between wage and price control authorities and consequently to tighter controls, there is no reason to believe that the inflationary trend as such occasioned the first wage and price agreement, as is often asserted in Austria. For before this agreement, as before each of the subsequent ones, an additional factor entered the picture: the demand of an economic sector other than labor and management for a larger share of the national

---

[2] Institut für Wirtschaftsforschung, *Monatsbericht*, October, 1946, p. 127.

product. In the case of the October, 1947, agreement, it was the demand of agriculture for substantially higher farm prices. The demand was recognized by competing economic organizations as justified in part; but coming at a time when the national product was wretchedly low, when many workers' incomes did not cover subsistence minima, when business had every reason to be deeply concerned about economic reconstruction and mass purchasing power, it created a situation clearly calling for a policy that accommodated the demands of the rival economic sectors. None of the existing, decentralized, policy-making organs could do this, and direct labor-management negotiation obviously could not. Willingness to negotiate and compromise was doubtless promoted by the common suffering and the further cut in production arising from a disastrous fuel shortage in the winter of 1946-47. Before Christmas this had occasioned a virtually complete industrial standstill. In mid-January 2,289 plants employing approximately 90,000 workers were still idle because of lack of coal.[3] With this bitter memory fresh and another winter approaching, the meager pie from which to cut profits, wages, farm income, pensions, and reconstruction was the paramount economic fact from the perspective of all participants.

NEGOTIATIONS PRIOR TO THE FIRST WAGE-PRICE AGREEMENT

Inspection of Table 1 suggests that food prices rose steeply in April and May of 1947. This posed a serious problem for pensioners and wage earners already at or below subsistence levels. Further unilateral wage demands would not have helped the unorganized and weakly organized who most needed additional purchasing power and would, in any case, have stimulated runaway inflation. Business groups similarly showed strong concern at this time over the uncoordinated wage and price developments and the inflationary danger.[4] Both sides accordingly welcomed the idea of general negotiations to supplement and perhaps replace the decentralized control pattern.[5]

Although the negotiations took place amid the greatest secrecy, the general position of each group and the procedure followed can be described.

The Trade Union Federation, Chamber of Labor, and Socialist Party groups placed primary emphasis on strict price controls and on wage increases sufficient to match the increase in living costs. In speeches, convention resolutions, and editorials in the *Arbeiter-Zeitung*, spokesmen for these organizations claimed that the standard

---

[3] Institut für Wirtschaftsforschung, *Monatsbericht*, December, 1946, pp. 69-71.
[4] *Das Kleine Volksblatt*, July 18 (1947), p. 2; July 20, p. 2.
[5] Both the Chamber of Labor and the Chamber of Trade claim the distinction of having originated the idea.

of living of workers was under the 1937 level by a wider margin than was true of farmers and that wages must consequently rise more than agricultural prices. To assure maintenance of real wages thereafter, labor and Socialist groups insisted upon effective rationing, production, and price controls, reduction in the quantity of currency in circulation, the forcing of business to release hoarded goods, particularly iron, and a change in the wage tax to prevent taxing away of the new wage increases.[6] Restiveness and strikes in July, following the food price increases, underscored the labor demands.

Both agriculture and business groups tended to soft-pedal rationing, production, and price controls and to oppose currency curtailment even more strongly. Spokesmen for these interests emphasized the need for an increase in production and productivity as a prerequisite to an improvement in living standards and insisted that prices be set high enough to cover costs.[7] They indicated willingness to go along with some cost-of-living wage boost. Although one agriculture statement blamed both labor and industry for allegedly raising wages and "the prices to cover them" without thinking of "the total economic effect,"[8] there was no public indication of differences between the business and the agriculture representatives in the negotiations.

With so many people at or under a subsistence living standard and the economic pie so meager, careful calculation of price trends and relative sacrifice seemed an indispensable preliminary to the final decisions. In a meeting on July 15 among top representatives of the three Chambers and the Trade Union Federation, it was agreed that a working committee of economists and statisticians representing these same organizations would undertake such computations, acting on the premise that both wages and industrial prices should be adjusted to the new agricultural price increases.

As all subsequent wage-price agreements were negotiated in their first stages in approximately the same manner, it is worth describing the nature of the computations which the economic technicians of the participating organizations completed in the next few days. The necessary farm price increases were calculated through to end prices, using the consumption pattern of the Institute of Economic Research's cost of living index. As it was estimated that this price rise plus necessary utility rate increases would raise the cost of living index to about 280, and as the hourly earnings index then stood at 204 (April, 1945 = 100 in both cases), an increase of 37 per cent in hourly earnings would be necessitated. Because such a wage increase would itself increase pro-

[6] Cf. *Arbeiterkammer Jahrbuch*, 1947, pp. 13-14; *Arbeiter-Zeitung*, July 20 (1947), pp. 1-2; July 25, p. 1; July 19, p. 1.
[7] *Das Kleine Volksblatt*, July 19 (1947), p. 2; July 18, p. 2; July 20, p. 2; July 23, p. 2.
[8] *Das Kleine Volksblatt*, July 26, 1947, p. 2.

duction costs, however, a second calculation of most important food prices, given the higher wages, was undertaken — assuming also a monthly increase of 52 schillings in the wages of skilled labor and of 48 schillings in the wages of unskilled and farm workers. This second calculation yielded a probable increase of 9 per cent in grains, 30 per cent in potatoes, 25 per cent in sugar beets, 11 per cent in milk, and 12 per cent in eggs, which satisfied the demands of the farmers. The food price index would thereby jump from 144.45 to 254.96 (1945 ceiling prices = 100) and the cost of living index to 294.7. It was now accordingly necessary to raise wages by an average of 45 per cent rather than 37 per cent. The agreed increases for lower income groups were actually somewhat greater and those for the better paid workers somewhat less.[9]

The top officers of the three Chambers and the Trade Union Federation took over the negotiations upon completion of these computations. Before a final agreement could be reached special discussions were necessary with some unions, especially those representing the farm workers and salaried workers in private industry. On July 21 President Karl Mantler of the Vienna Chamber of Labor drew up an eight-point proposal summarizing the principles on which it appeared agreement could be reached in view of the previous discussions, a document which served as the basis for the final agreement.

The final agreement fixed new prices for food, rent, coal, and public utilities, comprising together about 70 per cent of the expenditures of a worker family. Increases in pensions and wages, the latter averaging 45 per cent, but larger for those with low incomes and with special incentive increases for piece workers, were designed to compensate for this burden.

The working committee had not found it possible to establish a fixed relationship between wages and industrial prices, as had been done with respect to farm prices. To prevent increased costs from injuring production, businessmen in the uncontrolled portion of the economy, for which no other stabilization measures had been included, were told that effective August 1 they might increase prices so as to reflect cost increases, such price boosts to reflect the wage increases plus an additional amount varying inversely with the ratio of wage costs to total costs. Labor representatives contented themselves with a general right of protest against exorbitant development of individual prices and an agreement that if the cost of living index should climb more than 10 per cent above the level contemplated in the wage-price

---

[9] For the description of the computations by the working committee, I am indebted to Staribacher, *op. cit.*, pp. 52-53. Staribacher was himself a member of this committee and further clarified some of the negotiations for this and later pacts in an interview with the writer. Cf. also Institut für Wirtschaftsforschung, *Monatsbericht*, August, 1947, pp. 172-174.

pact, unions would be free after a three-month period to demand further increases. Until October 1, however, there was to be a moratorium on wage increases and on increases in the prices of any of the items in the stabilized 70 per cent sector.[10] An Economic Commission of representatives of the Trade Union Federation and the three Chambers was to maintain continuing surveillance of economic developments.

The whole agreement was laid before the Austrian Council of Ministers (Cabinet) on July 25 and unanimously adopted, hardly a surprising development in view of the fact that adherents of the same political parties and economic groups and many of the same individuals participated in both the negotiations and the Ministerial Council.

To effectuate those aspects of the pact calling for legislation, President Karl Renner summoned a special session of Parliament for July 30. The legislators quickly enacted a change in the income tax law to prevent the taxing away of most of the new wage increase, an increase in unemployment insurance commensurate with the estimated increase in living costs, and pension boosts of 70 per cent in some cases, two-thirds in others. As happened after all subsequent wage-price agreements as well, the Parliamentary debate consisted mostly of Communist attacks on the agreement as inadequately protecting workers against profiteers.[11]

The Chamber of Trade announced it planned to cooperate with the Chamber of Labor in maintaining continuing surveillance over observance of price ceilings,[12] a resolution which did not prevent President Julius Raab of the Chamber from announcing two months later that no business was required to give information to the Chamber of Labor, then seeking it in a price survey.[13]

---

[10] Institut für Wirtschaftsforschung, *Monatsbericht*, August, 1947, p. 174.
[11] *Arbeiter-Zeitung*, July 31, 1947, p. 1.
[12] *Das Kleine Volksblatt*, September 27, 1947, p. 2.
[13] *Ibid.*, November 23, 1947, p. 1.

CHAPTER 3 The Second Wage-Price Agreement

MONETARY REFORM

A significant price policy development involving an instructive clash of economic interests occurred on the subject of monetary reform immediately after conclusion of the first agreement. In an effort to prevent the compensatory wage boost from becoming illusory or worse, labor and Socialist groups intensified a campaign they had begun earlier in the year to secure a new and drastic reduction in the amount of currency in circulation. Money volume in October, 1947, was 27.6 billion schillings (11.4 billion in savings accounts), as against only 4.7 billion in 1937; but the official price level was only three times as great, production volume only 60 per cent as high, and currency circulation active as compared to 1937.[1] Clearly, here was an important source of price pressure.

The Austrian Institute of Economic Research pointed out in November, 1947, that the money surplus encouraged black market profiteering and goods hoarding, promoted uneconomic distribution of the labor force, and reduced incentive to work.[2] Labor and Socialist groups regarded the surplus with all the more disfavor because they saw most of the savings as having resulted from the Nazi financial economy and wartime profits.[3] The business world, on the other hand, was reluctant to permit sweeping reform, although not unanimously so. The Association of Austrian Industrialists, representing heavy industry, financial groups, and leaders in the money and credit section of the Chamber of Trade, were in opposition, with few exceptions, evidently fearing this would be the prelude to tight governmental controls over money and credit. The labor section of the People's Party and some of the top leadership of the Chamber of Trade were more conscious of the inflationary dangers, particularly as the cost of living index was already 16 per cent higher in November than it had been just after the August wage-price agreement. Agreement on sweeping legislation was finally achieved in the government. A neat summary of

---

[1] Institut für Wirtschaftsforschung, *Monatsbericht,* November, 1947, p. 272.
[2] *Ibid.,* p. 271.
[3] Cf. *Arbeiter-Zeitung* editorial, November 22, 1947, pp. 1-2; *Arbeiterkammer Jahrbuch,* 1947, pp. 370-371.

the delicate balance of power on the issue within the business world appears between the lines of a statement in Parliament by Julius Raab, president of the Chamber of Trade: "Just as the People's Party has never shunned responsibility, she takes co-responsibility for this law."[4]

Because the Russian element in the Allied Council delayed its approval of the fiscal law, almost three weeks went by between its passage by the Parliament and its effective date, arousing some intense resentment against this interference with domestic policy and incidentally permitting some persons partially to evade the measure's disadvantages by paying their debts in a hurry.

The statute provided for the exchange of old schillings for new at a three-to-one ratio,[5] fully extinguished savings accounts dating from the war period without compensation except that the needy were permitted to retain a sum of from 2,500 to 3,500 schillings, and transformed funds in the limited use accounts of the December, 1945, schilling law into 2 per cent federal bonds. New accounts were left alone, though partially blocked for three to six months. A tax on goods to place part of the burden on property, as distinguished from money, was shelved until a later time.[6]

Compared to most measures attempted by those who seek to pit themselves against the bewildering economic forces of the modern day, this one was spectacularly successful. The price-wage spiral straightened out and throughout most of 1948 reached horizontally toward what was hoped was a stabilized future. Black market prices tumbled fast. As early as January, 1948, the Institute of Economic Research was hailing a greater supply of goods through a decline in hoarding.[7] And students of social science were able to learn from the process how the various economic organizations, particularly the Chamber of Trade, would line up on a policy placing the advantages of price control ahead of the disadvantages of governmental interference with money and credit.

ECONOMIC AND POLITICAL SETTING

The fiscal reform and the first wage-price agreement thus set the stage for some welcome economic developments in 1948 — all the more welcome because the Austrian standard of living in December, 1947, was among the lowest in Europe, and industrial goods were either

---

[4] *Das Kleine Volksblatt*, November 21, 1947, p. 2. Cf. also "Denkschrift der Vereinigung Österreichischer Industrieller zur Währungsfrage," Vienna, June, 1947, and editorials in *Das Kleine Volksblatt* and *Die Arbeiter-Zeitung, passim.*
[5] Each person could exchange 150 schillings at one-to-one.
[6] Institut für Wirtschaftsforschung, *Monatsbericht*, November, 1947, pp. 272-273.
[7] *Ibid.*, January, 1948, pp. 2-3.

too expensive to buy or not available.[8] After rising in the first few months following the August, 1947, agreement, official prices levelled off early in the year and remained level. Unions refrained from asking for wage increases even though the initial price rise had carried the gap between the cost of living index and the hourly earnings index beyond the 10 per cent foreseen in the agreement. Before the monetary reform, black market prices had averaged five times official prices; but between December, 1947, and May, 1948, black market food prices plunged from an index of 4,700 (March, 1938 = 100) to 1,400, according to the Institute of Economic Research. Between August, 1947, and August, 1948, production and productivity rose 43.5 per cent and 23.8 per cent, respectively. The food ration was increased in June, and many commodities were removed from the rationed list during the year.

Although the moratorium on inflation and the decline of the black market would normally have tended to lessen the likelihood of further wage-price agreements, it was the latter, oddly enough, that started events moving toward the second agreement, proving once again both the absence and the meaninglessness of "normality." The spectacular decline in black market food prices had cut the total income of farmers about 60 per cent by May,[9] generating enormous pressure for further aid to agriculture, particularly as internal farm prices were still well below world market prices and the increases of 1947 had not been adequate to cover the farmers' costs. Without especially emphasizing the precise reason for their new sense of urgency, the farm organizations began asking for price increases right after the fiscal reform. To their verbal demands they added the tried tactic of holding down milk deliveries, with the result that market deliveries in April, 1948, were only 87 per cent of the 1947 average. In an attempt to cope with this situation without a new rise in living costs, the government agreed, effective April 1, to add a subsidy of 50 groschen per liter to the producer price of milk. Shortly thereafter subsidies were also placed on bread grains, oats, maize, and potatoes, adding up to an average increase in farm income of 68 per cent on plant products and 66 per cent on animal products. These increased prices were still below both world market prices and what agriculture wanted. The farm groups also began immediately to demand that the subsidies be transformed into higher consumer prices as insurance that later producer price increases would not have to be used to cut the subsidies.[10] This de-

---

[8] *Ibid.*, December, 1947, p. 310.

[9] Joseph Staribacher, "Ziele und Möglichkeiten der behördlichen Preisbildung und die Preisbildung in Österreich seit 1945" (Ph.D. dissertation, Vienna, 1950), p. 63.

[10] There is an instructive analogy here with the distaste of American farmer organizations for the Brannan Plan.

mand was a major reason for the second wage-price agreement in August.[11]

At a conference of the presidents of the Chambers of Agriculture on September 10 the agriculture position in the October, 1948, negotiations was agreed upon. It consisted principally of insistence that higher prices be fixed for farm products, thereby transferring the subsidy burden from government to consumers. The farm organizations calculated that abolition of all price supports would make necessary an 8 per cent general wage increase. They strongly opposed any larger increase for labor on the ground it would lead to increased agricultural production costs. Tax reductions were favored.[12]

Although labor could muster arguments in the summer of 1948 for a higher share of the national income, it is extremely doubtful that wage demands would have occasioned a new general agreement in the absence of the new upturn in food prices these agriculture demands contemplated. The gap between the cost of living index and the hourly earnings index was 20.5 per cent in March, 1948, but in later months it declined to 15.8 per cent, thanks partly to some negotiated wage increases in the late spring and summer. Net income rose somewhat faster than hourly earnings as a result of overtime, and overemployment and an increase in the labor force boosted family income, though very unevenly.

On the other hand, the decline in the black market had not been an unalloyed blessing for labor. After the end of the war it had been a common practice for employers to give their workers goods in addition to wages and salaries. These commodities were usually sold on the black market and served as a necessary safety valve against unrealistic wage controls and official wage-price relations. To this extent the drop in black market prices meant a loss in wage earner income which the Institute of Economic Research described as "a very real factor."[13] As for real income, the Institute estimated in August, 1948, that it had risen since the first wage-price agreement, though perhaps not in the degree justified by production, productivity, and profit trends.[14]

Throughout 1948 the labor and Socialist organizations demanded price cuts through the voluntary action of sellers and through stepped-up government enforcement of the price control law. Repeatedly labor leaders emphasized that they much preferred price reduction to wage increases, but hinted that the latter would be sought unless the cost

---

[11] Staribacher, *op. cit.*, pp. 63-73; Institut für Wirtschaftsforschung, *Monatsbericht*, July, 1948, p. 258.
[12] *Das Kleine Volksblatt*, September 11, 1948, p. 1.
[13] Institut für Wirtschaftsforschung, *Monatsbericht*, August, 1948, p. 284. In interviews labor people frequently emphasized the importance of this development.
[14] *Ibid.*, p. 284.

of living were reduced.[15] When late summer brought no reduction in food prices, but rather the farm demand for increases, the labor and Socialist groups demanded a general compensatory wage increase plus an additional increase to reflect labor's contribution to the rise in productivity.[16] Once again both agriculture and labor favored fairly substantial changes in the status quo, with far-reaching consequences for business, consumers, and the public budget.

Another general wage-price agreement was the obvious way out. In the negotiations, the labor organizations attacked the agriculture position all along the line, arguing that price supports should be retained for consumer protection, that farmers should try to bolster their income through increased production and fair deliveries to the cities rather than price demands, and that the workers were entitled to far more than the 8 per cent to which the Chambers of Agriculture were willing to agree if price supports were abandoned. The labor groups proposed that food price supports be continued and paid out of an increase in the payroll tax to be met by employers, and they favored calculation of living costs by taking a four-person family as the standard. During the negotiations labor publications and speeches several times charged that far from seeking stabilization, business groups were deliberately using the agriculture demands as a lever to start prices rising again.[17]

As nearly as can be ascertained, the Chamber of Trade placed most emphasis on opposing further wage increases or keeping them as low as possible. Evidently there was considerable divergence in viewpoint between the labor and the business sections within the People's Party. In several articles and statements the chairman of the Labor Section, representing chiefly white collar workers, urged that the real income of workers be raised, that the policy of increasing the lower wages faster be reversed in order to favor white collar workers, and that children's allowances and family subsidies be continued. The business spokesmen, who were much more influential, emphasized wage stability and the discontinuance of price supports and rationing as quickly as possible, and flatly refused to accept the labor proposal for a payroll tax to cover the agricultural subsidies. According to leaders of the Trade Union Federation, business representatives in the nego-

---

[15] Cf. articles and editorials in *Arbeiter-Zeitung*, August 5 (1948), October 3, August 25, and *passim*; *Arbeiterkammer Jahrbuch*, 1948, pp. 198-217, 244-250, 474-479; Institut für Wirtschaftsforschung, *Monatsbericht*, February, 1948, pp. 45-46.

[16] A schilling devaluation intensified both agricultural and labor concern.

[17] *Arbeiter-Zeitung*, August 25 (1948), September 16, August 5, August 29, October 3; Institut für Wirtschaftsforschung, *Monatsbericht*, September, 1948, p. 238; *Arbeiterkammer Jahrbuch*, 1948, *op. cit.* A two-head family with two children was finally used as the basis for calculating living costs.

tiations offered to support a 10 per cent general wage increase if prices were allowed to rise.[18]

Although a great deal of jockeying for position had thus been going on for a long time, formal negotiations started on September 7 and agreement on the fundamental issues was achieved on September 15. The labor organizations settled for a general 6 per cent wage increase even though the cost of living had risen almost 16 per cent since the first agreement. Price supports on meat, fat, milk, and milk products were abandoned, and each worker was granted a 34 schilling monthly food subsidy to be paid by employers. The subsidy was intended to compensate for the resulting increases in the prices of these necessities. The price supports on grain and potatoes remained, chiefly because business was unwilling to assume a greater burden without a general industrial price boost, to which labor in turn objected. Workers were also to benefit from a 23 schilling monthly allowance for each child and dependent, to come out of the public till.

The negotiators calculated that the rise in prices of foods no longer to be supported would mean a 14.9 per cent increase in the cost of living. As the net wage increase (counting the food subsidy and children's allowances for a four-person family with two children) would be 21.7 per cent, labor would experience an improvement in real income of 6.8 per cent *if* industrial and other prices remained unchanged — a dubious assumption. The gap between the cost of living index and the hourly earnings index would thus be cut from 15.8 per cent to 9.3 per cent.

This second wage-price agreement was designed, then, to ameliorate low standards of living among farmers and wage earners, the costs to be met by employers and the government almost equally.[19] It continued the policy of equalizing wages by granting relatively higher increases to low-income families. The Austrian Institute of Economic Research declared that favorable production and productivity developments justified the assumption that industry as a whole could bear its new burden with equanimity, but warned that some businesses with small profit margins or high ratios of labor costs to total costs would find it extremely difficult, a point emphatically proclaimed by some business spokesmen as well. The Institute also feared that the agreement would widen the gap between cost-covering prices and world

---

[18] *Das Kleine Volksblatt*, September 3 (1948), p. 2; September 11, p. 1; September 9, p. 1; *Arbeiter-Zeitung*, August 31 (1948), pp. 1-2; September 16, p. 2.

[19] Although abandonment of some farm price subsidies meant a saving for the government, children's allowances and increases in the salaries of public employees more than outweighed this.

market prices, possibly with unfavorable consequences for Austrian exports.[20]

After conclusion of each wage-price agreement, meetings were arranged by the Socialist faction of the Trade Union Federation to explain the new wage and price provisions to Socialist works-councilors.[21] In no case were these meetings devoted exclusively to loud hosannas for the negotiators, and the one held in Vienna on September 17, 1948, was no exception. Although most of the councilors agreed that the negotiators had done as well as possible and produced an acceptable agreement, there was clearly a widespread fear that future price increases would endanger the slim wage gain. The most violent denunciations were reserved, however, for the Communists (who had opposed the agreement with the argument that the wage increase was much too small) and the farmers, who were blamed for their price demands and the resulting threats to economic stability.[22] •

Editorials in the People's Party–Chamber of Trade newspaper praised the agreement and claimed credit for the idea of children's allowances. It reminded readers that business was assuming new burdens to protect stability.[23]

---

[20] On the provisions and significance of the second wage-price agreement, see Institut für Wirtschaftsforschung, *Monatsbericht*, September, 1948, pp. 321-327; Staribacher, *op. cit.*, pp. 77-82; Stephan Wirlandner, "Ein Stabilisierungsversuch," *Die Zukunft*, October, 1948, p. 291.

[21] The Austrian works-councilor corresponds somewhat to the American shop steward. He is nominated by a political party, however, and elected by the workers in his plant. The Socialists consistently have greater success than the other parties in these elections.

[22] *Arbeiter-Zeitung*, September 18, 1948, pp. 1-2.

[23] The labor organizations would have preferred a larger wage increase. The allowances were a compromise. *Das Kleine Volksblatt*, September 17, 1948, p. 2.

ECONOMIC SETTING

During the month of October the cost of living rose 18.6 per cent as a result of the price provisions of the second agreement, an increase that somewhat surpassed the 14.9 per cent calculated by the negotiators. Subsequent economic trends were more reassuring, for prices rose only very slightly in November and December and declined somewhat thereafter until the third wage-price agreement in May, displaying a seasonal trend for the first time since the war. Black market food prices usually moved in the same directions as official prices during this period, only more so. In November they experienced a 10 per cent rise as a result of rumors of an impending currency reform, the first upswing since December, 1947; but in the new year they dropped quickly to new lows. By mid-March they had fallen 28 per cent from the December high and were not very far above official food prices. Wages changed little, the hourly earnings index remaining somewhat more than 10 per cent under the cost of living index. By March, 1949, there were some signs of wage increase demands, especially among public employees and others who felt they had been left behind in the September, 1948, agreement.[1]

An interesting, if unconvincing, effort at nongovernmental price control occurred during the early months of 1949. The Economic Commission, representing the three Chambers and the Trade Union Federation, issued lists of prevailing prices in the various markets for chocolate, cocoa, almonds, raisins, and hazelnuts, and the administrative office of each local market did the same for fruits and vegetables. These lists were intended to exert a psychological influence. It was recognized that only substantial price violations were punished legally. As has been seen, prices did remain stable during this period, but it is doubtful that they would have been any less so if no such lists had been available.[2]

A relatively severe increase in unemployment occurred during the winter of 1948 chiefly as the result of sharply reduced construction activity — unwelcome confirmation of the fact that Austria's economy

---

[1] The summary of economic developments is based chiefly on the Institut für Wirtschaftsforschung's *Monatsberichte* for the months between October, 1948, and April, 1949.
[2] *Ibid.*, March, 1949, p. 91.

had sufficiently recovered from its postwar trauma to experience seasonal fluctuations again.

The third wage-price agreement, of May-June, 1949, was negotiated and became effective during and following a period in which prices remained steady. As always, the immediate impetus for the agreement arose neither from a business boost in industrial prices nor from wage demands, but from a third claimant on the national income — in this case beneficiaries of a solvent public budget, which would include farmers and pensioners. Such aid was imperiled in the spring of 1949 by an ominous and growing deficit in the governmental budget, amounting in May to approximately 2.5 billion schillings. Government salaries had not kept pace with the cost of living, and federal employees were now demanding a thirteenth month's pay as a bonus. Occupation costs and the government's share of price and import subsidies were other heavy burdens. The problem was further aggravated by American pressure for measures that would permit reduction or abolition of food price supports financed from Marshall aid without internal economic dislocations. Business was not inclined to oppose these cuts, for they would afford an opportunity to place domestic economic relations on a "normal" basis and therefore eliminate governmental planning and restrictions on prices, production, and wage bargaining. The budget deficit was itself a bar to internal economic order which business groups could be expected to eye restively. Business was therefore willing to negotiate, but sought to keep wage increases to a minimum, arguing that this agreement would mean little or no increase in industrial prices — a claim disputed by labor and, somewhat less forcefully, by the Institute of Economic Research.

As for labor and Socialist groups, the threat to governmental pensions, fear that substantial declines in governmental spending would aggravate unemployment, the opportunity to place the chief burden of the inevitable wage-price readjustment on business, and a chance to get industrial pensions for retired workers made the prospect of a new agreement palatable, even at the cost of some cut in real wages; but labor fought cuts in food subsidies. On the last point a Chamber of Labor economist who participated in the negotiations wrote later that unions forewent greater wage demands ". . . from the insight that wage increases . . . if an inflationary development was to be prevented . . . dared not be greater than the productivity increase for all plants." Especially in the export industries labor negotiators took into account the fact that cost increases and sinking world market prices limited ability to increase either prices or wages.[3]

---

[3] Joseph Staribacher, "Ziele und Möglichkeiten der behördlichen Preisbildung und die Preisbildung in Österreich seit 1945" (Ph.D. dissertation, Vienna, 1950), pp. 91-92.

Agriculture organizations had long favored elimination of Marshall food subsidies in return for higher retail food prices. In the negotiations, its representatives sought price increases for meat and grain products, with partial success.

PROVISIONS OF THE AGREEMENT

Provisions of the third agreement were made known in May and went into effect June 1. A major step toward relieving the Treasury was the imposition of an occupational cost tax in the form of a 20 per cent income tax increase. Because the income tax structure stemmed from the Nazi period, however, and was not consistently progressive, the income tax schedules also had to be changed to produce a graded, structure more in line with ability to pay. In addition, agricultural taxes were increased as were various excises, notably on sales, salt, alcoholic spirits, beer, wine, insurance, and mineral oil. Railroad, gas, electricity, and postal rates were boosted. Cuts in the number of public employees and in the number of war injury pensions further helped the budget outlook. The government's contribution to the social insurance fund was raised, however, from 25 to 30 per cent of all social security payments.

Subsidies on imports and agricultural products were cut substantially, entailing retail price increases for bread, flour, pork, milk, sugar, salt, beer, grits, and coal. Subsidies remained on coal, medicines, leather, grains, fodder, fertilizer, and fats.

On the improbable assumption that the prices of other goods and services would not be affected by these increases, it was calculated that the cost of living would rise 13.7 per cent, but the new take-home wages established by the agreement failed to compensate for even this optimistic figure. All workers received a flat 4.5 per cent increase. The 34-schilling food subsidy was replaced by increases of 30 groschen per hour for wage earners and 60 schillings per month for salaried personnel, with corresponding boosts for pensioners. The children's allowance rose from 23 to 37 schillings per child. But when the bite of the 20 per cent occupational tax and higher social insurance contributions had been digested, a net wage increase of only 3.3 per cent for single workers and 10.2 per cent for married ones remained, assuming a monthly wage of 677 schillings or salary of 830 schillings. Real wages were therefore reduced. A major long-term gain for labor realized in the third agreement was the establishment of old-age pensions for wage-earners in private industry comparable to those already received by white collar workers. Increased costs to the industrial sector were unquestionably greater than the reduction in real wages, but both wages and prices could and did move upward unevenly in periods between general wage-price agreements. Any comparison of burdens would accordingly be misleading.

Like the other agreements, the third represented a temporarily successful readjustment of burdens among the economic sectors to satisfy a pressing claim from an important segment of the population. As usual, it was popular with almost nobody, but it was stoutly defended by the chief parties as necessary in the circumstances. Labor officials expressed the view that general agreements hold wages down to those the least efficient producers can pay. Minister of Social Affairs Karl Maisel told a meeting of Socialist officers and works councilors: "We hope that this hard measure will be the last sacrifice that will finally bring our economy back to normal."[4] The works councilors proved less than enthusiastic, though they voted to approve the agreement.[5] Several protested that they should have been informed of the proposed changes before the final stage of the negotiations. One asserted it was "a wage agreement, but not a price agreement." Most of their resentment was reserved, however, for farmers, Communist demagogy, and the People's Party.[6] Meanwhile, the president of the Chamber of Trade argued in the Chamber's journal that it was "in the nature of the thing" that most of the burden should fall on business, for the only alternative was the "unholy course" of inflation. He tried to soothe his constituents by pointing to concomitant legislation (really part of the over-all bargain), which established lower tax rates on business earnings plowed into investments. But a few months later he was "reliably quoted" to the effect that the Chamber would enter into no more general agreements.[7]

---

[4] *Arbeiter-Zeitung,* May 8, 1949, p. 2.
[5] After each agreement had been negotiated, Socialist officials asked for a vote of confidence at a meeting of Socialist works councilors.
[6] *Arbeiter-Zeitung,* May 8, 1949, p. 2.
[7] *Das Kleine Volksblatt,* May 13, 1949, p. 2; ECA, *Monthly Labor Report,* October, 1949, p. 1.

ECONOMIC SETTING

Between the third wage-price agreement, of May, 1949, and the outbreak of the war in Korea in June, 1950, the Austrian economy almost achieved enough stability to make it seem likely that no more general agreements would be necessary. By October, 1949, black market prices in Vienna were only 30 per cent above official prices. There were secondary price effects of the third agreement, especially on goods with inelastic demands, and the cost of living index did rise somewhat faster than the index of hourly earnings in the second half of the year. But many unions were able to negotiate "transitional aid" increases on an industry basis in December, and these partially compensated for the gap, which was higher than it had been before the general agreement in May. In the winter the unemployment figure surpassed that of the previous year, reaching 195,000 in mid-February. During the first half of 1950 price changes were in general slightly downward. Production and productivity improved in highly encouraging fashion through this period. In June many unions were still restive because of the continuing gap between trends in wages and cost of living, despite the price declines; but without a Korean War this dissatisfaction could almost certainly have been dealt with through negotiation by the individual unions.

Politically, Austria was about as uninvolved in the Korean dispute as it was possible to be, for she was without an army, occupied by both Russia and the Western Powers, still not a member of the United Nations, and very likely rather "neutralist" in sentiment had she been in a position to make a choice. Economically, Austria was almost immediately and unfortunately affected, for the upsurge in prices on the world market destroyed her painfully achieved economic stability and rendered another general domestic economic readjustment necessary within three months. By September foreign raw materials were growing scarce, demand for goods was up, the buyers' market had become a sellers' market, wage increase demands were sharper, and unemployment had fallen to an unseasonable degree. In this situation the stepped-up pressure from the American MEC Mission[1] precipitated the fourth wage-price agreement, which went into effect on October 1.

In the early months of 1950, the MEC Mission had again initiated conversations with Austrian government representatives regarding the removal of all import subsidies and by July 1, 1950, "met with some resistance from about all quarters."[2] Bread grain subsidies were the chief stumbling block, for the unions stoutly opposed food price increases, later agreeing reluctantly only on condition that a general wage-price agreement accompany the shift to higher prices. An arrangement under which ECA continued to supply essential foods at the more favorable rate of exchange that had existed before the schilling devaluation of November, 1949, expired on June 30. In September the Mission reported that "all participants in the negotiations seemed to be reconciled to the probability that any reasonably satisfactory solution would have to include a new wage-price agreement."[3]

As usual, the Chamber of Trade made few positive demands, seeking rather to hold as much as possible of what it had secured through increases in production, productivity, and prices. Editorials in its journals and statements of its leaders concentrated on these objectives: (1) grant farmers relief through some increase in grain prices, but do not abandon subsidies altogether; (2) keep the compensating wage increase as low as possible; (3) reverse the trend toward equalization of wages. In the final days of negotiations the Chamber did begin to press for a reduction in the municipal mercantile tax, but this objective was not realized until later.

The chief labor-Socialist objective was to hold agricultural price increases to a minimum, although there was no inclination to argue that such increases were unnecessary. The original agriculture demands with regard to wheat and rye prices were denounced as exorbitant in view of what the economy could stand and the prevailing living standards for labor, although even these demands would not have brought internal prices up to world market levels. This was easily the knottiest question before the negotiators, and agreement was eventually reached on prices substantially below those first asked. On wheat, for example, the price finally set was 1.35 schillings per kilogram although the Chamber of Agriculture had first asked for 1.85. Before the agreement, wheat had sold for .85 schillings.

---

[1] In Austria the Mutual Security Administration was called the "Mission for Economic Cooperation" (MEC) because no military aid was involved. Food subsidies were technically paid out of the domestic budget and Marshall aid used for reconstruction activities, but this was actually a bookkeeping device to satisfy American insistence that the Marshall Plan was intended only for long-term reconstruction. Without the Marshall Plan it is doubtful that the subsidies would have been possible, and the government was under constant pressure to reduce them against the day outside help would end.

[2] Mission for Economic Cooperation, *Monthly Labor Report No. 8,* June, 1950.

[3] Mission for Economic Cooperation, *Monthly Labor Reports Nos. 10 and 11,* August and September, 1950.

Throughout the year the labor-Socialist groups had urged stricter price controls and lower prices, and in the negotiations they sought assurance that there would be no subsequent increases in industrial prices. No formal provision to this effect was included, although the industry and commerce representatives assured the public that there would not be secondary price effects. As always, the Trade Union Federation insisted upon compensatory wage increases to cover increases in living costs resulting from the agreement. As usual, the Chamber of Trade agreed in principle, but fought to limit the amount sought, arguing that the cost of living index was unreliable and that interim wage increases had already compensated to some extent.[4]

Finally, officials of the Trade Union Federation and the Socialist Party were keenly aware that they faced a problem in persuading their members and the public generally that it was necessary and justifiable to enter into another wage-price agreement entailing no increase in real wages and every probability of a decrease. The denouement of the fourth agreement suggests that the dimensions of this problem were underestimated, but speeches to union and Socialist gatherings and articles in the labor and party press did try to prepare the membership for this agreement more carefully than had been done for any of the previous ones.

Negotiations among representatives of the three Chambers and the Trade Union Federation lasted for weeks. On September 22, the Ministerial Council began to consider their recommendations, and agreement was finally reached on September 26 — the pact to become effective October 1.

PROVISIONS OF THE AGREEMENT

Although the money expended on subsidies was cut in half, some supports were maintained on artificial fertilizer, fats, wheat, and feed corn and very small supports on sugar, gas, medicines, and hides.[5] Increases in producers' prices for wheat, rye, and sugar beets and increases in retail prices for bread, flour, sugar, house coal, electricity, and transportation were provided.[6]

To compensate for the resulting increase in living costs, all wages and salaries were increased 10 per cent or at least 100 schillings per

---

[4] Cf. *Die Wiener Handelkammer*, September 30, 1950, pp. 1-3; also editorials in *Die Neue Wiener Tageszeitung*, September 17, 1951, and July 25, 1950, p. 1.

[5] MSA agreed to continue to provide the necessary funds for these reduced subsidies, though it also continued to press for their complete elimination as quickly as possible.

[6] One reliable report had it that the increases in retail food prices were higher than necessary because the negotiators had tentatively taken excessive processors' requests at face value, intending later to determine how these would affect farmers and workers; but because the government was eager to announce an agreement and thereby allay rumors and business uncertainty, these requests were prematurely announced as granted in full. Cf. Mission for Economic Cooperation, "Economic Implications of the Wage-Price Agreement of September, 1950," typewritten, pp. 24-25.

month, the latter alternative further equalizing the wage structure. The government food subsidy for children was increased from 37 to 60 schillings per child per month. Pensioners got a monthly increase of 50 schillings if single and 80 schillings if married. The ceiling for calculation of social insurance contributions was raised to 1,500 schillings from 1,050, however, and all increases were subject to existing wage tax provisions.

The Institute of Economic Research as well as business groups, labor groups, and American economic observers in MEC agreed that the immediate burden of the agreement would fall on business groups. Broken down into the components of industrial production, the agreement meant a 13 per cent jump in labor costs, 25 per cent in electricity costs, and 7 per cent in the cost of raw materials. This added up to an increase of 10.1 per cent in total production costs in the construction industry, 7.8 per cent in the iron and steel industry, 9.4 per cent in mining, and 5.1 per cent in textiles.[7] While making much of the fact that the pact would saddle business with a heavier load, spokesmen for the Chamber of Trade and the People's Party vigorously defended the agreement, saying, "The consequences would be even more unbearable if the burden were refused."[8]

Far more critical, it turned out, was the reception of the pact by workers. The price increases, with the threat they carried of cuts in real wages when secondary price boosts were completed, came as a great shock to most people. There was little doubt that with workers and consumers this agreement was even less popular than the previous ones had been. The Communists conducted a vigorous campaign, denouncing the pact and the alleged encouragement it gave to "price usurers" and demanding very large wage increases.

COMMUNIST ATTEMPT AT A COUP D'ÉTAT

This line was unquestionably popular in many quarters. The Communists took sufficient encouragement from its reception to attempt a general strike and, if possible, a coup d'état upon announcement of the terms of the agreement. On September 26, the Communists, with the support of the extreme right-wing League of Independents, proclaimed a general strike. The strike's principal impact was felt in Linz, Austria's leading steel-producing center. Here an oven was dampened off, and at about 11 o'clock in the morning approximately 1,000 strikers marched to the Chamber of Labor building and occupied it, ousting the Socialist officials who had their offices there. Toward

---

[7] *Ibid.*, p. 26.
[8] *Die Wiener Handelkammer*, October 14, 1950, p. 9.

evening, disturbances at the railroad station interrupted traffic to Vienna. Even at this center of strike activity, however, the successes of the Communists were short-lived. Additional recruits for the strike failed to materialize. At 9:30 p.m. a company of police reoccupied the Chamber of Labor building and train service was restored within about an hour after it had been stopped.

In Graz the 2,000 workers of one big factory struck and began a parade, but when the Provincial Governor appealed to them to return to work, they did so. A sit-down strike in a plant in Styria lasted several hours, and there were sporadic strikes in Lower Austria.

In Vienna there was no active support for the strike outside the Soviet zone of the city. Work was halted at the Russian-operated "USIA" plants, and Russian MP's often appeared at the site of demonstrations. For a time, passing automobiles were forced to park across important intersections so as to hold up street cars and other traffic, but as the population did not take part and showed no enthusiasm for the activity, the streets were opened again shortly. One incident at a construction site on the Simmeringer Hauptstrasse aptly reflected the prevailing mood once it was clear that the strike was a Communist vehicle. When Communist demonstrators appeared there and vigorously urged the construction workers to join in a general strike, the answer was, "Leave us alone. We're on piece work." The conclusion is inescapable that the Chamber of Trade and the Trade Union Federation were correct in their claims that the coup was averted by worker resistance to the Communist strategy rather than by police action. Indeed, very little of the latter occurred at all, owing in part to the long-standing opposition of the Russian High Commissioner in Austria to the arming of the Austrian police.[9]

The Communist leaders evidently decided, however, that something might still be done to exploit the dissatisfaction with the fourth agreement, for the Communist Party called a meeting of "all Austrian works councilors" for September 30, and those who attended agreed upon another general strike attempt for October 4. A conference of Viennese Socialist works councilors on October 3 unanimously voted *against* the general strike and denounced the Communist aims and methods in that violent language which Social Democrats reserve for Communists. President Karl Böhm of the Trade Union Federation told this meeting that high wage increases such as those demanded by the Communists would bring economic chaos, which was the real Communist goal.

The October 4 strike proved an even greater fiasco than its predecessor a week earlier. Except for some minor disturbances in the Soviet

---

[9] *Neue Wiener Tageszeitung*, September 27 and 28, 1950; *Arbeiter-Zeitung*, September 28, 1950.

zone and a sparsely attended strike meeting in front of the Vienna City Hall, all remained normal.[10]

In the first meeting of the Executive Committee of the Trade Union Federation after the Communist strikes, President Böhm announced that the unions were "forced to expel or release from their offices all those members whose actions violated the rules of the unions laid down in their constitutions." Vice-President Gottlieb Fiala, long the Communist representative on the Executive Committee, had already been expelled by his union, the Textile Workers. Equally significant was the announcement that four officials of the Food Workers Union had been expelled from the Communist Party for failure to follow the party line just prior to or immediately after the fourth wage-price agreement.[11]

The United States Mission for Economic Cooperation in Vienna reported that as explanations of the need for substantial reductions in subsidies were made to union shop stewards, "public sentiment gradually changed from one of hostility toward union and political leaders to hostility toward the Communists." Socialist leaders of the Trade Union Federation were keenly aware of the precarious character of their position, however. Immediately after the general strike attempts, President Böhm and Secretary-Treasurer Anton Proksch appealed to the Mission for funds for public construction and an apprentice training program in order to curtail unemployment, warning that failure to do so would be playing into the hands of the Communists.[12]

---

[10] *Neue Wiener Tageszeitung,* October 5, 1950; *Arbeiter-Zeitung,* October 4 and 5, 1950.
[11] Mission for Economic Cooperation, *Monthly Labor Report No. 14,* December 21, 1950.
[12] There are those in the Austrian trade union movement who suggest that in evaluating appeals of this type, it is well to remember that foreigners have learned that American diplomats are inordinately sensitive to threats of a Communist danger.

CHAPTER 6

The Fifth Wage-Price Agreement

ECONOMIC SETTING

At the time of the conclusion of the fourth agreement, the Austrian people had just undergone many weeks of unnerving rumors regarding the wage-price negotiations in progress and their probable dire effects on the cost of living. Korea then meant the beginning of materials shortages, an excellent chance that living would become more difficult, and some chance of a third world war. Above all, it meant uncertainty about immediate economic change as well as about the future of world politics. In this atmosphere it was easy for the announcements of actual price increases to create restiveness and some hesitancy before rejecting the Communist effort to consummate a *Putsch.*

In the succeeding months Korea came to mean a highly dynamic economy, with rising wages as well as prices, goods shortages, and the prospect of continuing for an indefinite time as a localized "police action," with a clear implication that Austrian economic policy must adjust from month to month. The emphasis in statements from organized economic groups was placed now on a continuing effort to win optimum gains in the shifting battle of prices, wages, taxes, and influence in governmental bodies. No longer did the workers see any particular act as a conclusive blow which could elevate or depress their position for long.

Almost immediately after the fourth agreement prices and wages began chasing each other in an uneven spiral in which it was impossible to distinguish secondary price effects of the September, 1950, agreement from the effects of rising raw material costs. Between November, 1950, and May, 1951, the cost of living index jumped 38.7 percentage points and the index of hourly earnings rose 34.5 points for single workers and 44.5 points for workers reaping the benefit of allowances for two children. The wage rises came from negotiations initiated by unions in individual industries: shoes and dressmaking as early as December; graphics, cement, glass, paper goods, leather goods, textiles and others soon thereafter. By May about 80 per cent of the workers had secured increases of 10 to 12 per cent beyond the level reached in the fourth wage-price agreement. The movement was not limited to the well-organized industrial sectors and represented a general rise rather than a catch-up for the particularly depressed. Increases were especially favorable, however, in the export industries, flourishing now because of the resurrected world-wide arms economy.

Between the fourth agreement, in September, 1950, and the fifth, in May, 1951, the trend of both production and productivity was encouragingly upward, with minor dips occasionally. In the late spring of 1951, however, production dropped somewhat because of increasingly serious raw material shortages. Unemployment reached serious proportions in December and January, even surpassing the level of the previous winter, but declined rapidly after mid-January because of emergency programs and an upturn in construction work.[1]

The new situation with respect to demand for, and supply of, raw materials created a lively concern among the various economic groups regarding government organization for controlling production, distribution, and sale of these materials. Because decisions in this area had a clear impact on prices, employment, and wages, they must be viewed as part of the process of wage-price policy formation with which the present paper is concerned.

The basic fact was that there was now a strong foreign demand for Austrian raw materials and a diminished supply (at greatly increased prices) of those goods which Austria had to buy abroad. The large Austrian lumber industry, for example, could clearly benefit by selling abroad at the price of a reduced supply of lumber for domestic industry and consumption. The already limited supply of foreign exchange shrank substantially because of the increase in world prices.

With the stakes of foreign trade and exchange policy high for all economic sectors, a battle quickly shaped up over the organization to formulate policy in this area. Labor wanted government controls over disposition of raw materials and a voice in shaping the controls. Business groups understandably preferred freedom to handle this trade as they pleased and opposed government intervention — which, in effect, meant labor, agriculture, and consumer intervention. There was even an occasional hint that business preferred to have as little interference by farm groups as possible and that intra-People's Party clashes on the issue were not unknown.[2]

CONFLICT OVER ECONOMIC CONTROL LAWS

As early as November, 1950, Minister of Nationalized Industry Karl Waldbrunner urged at a Socialist meeting in Graz that controls

---

[1] The review of economic trends is based upon the *Monatsberichte* of the Institut für Wirtschaftsforschung.
[2] See *Arbeiter-Zeitung*, March 16, 1951, pp. 1-2.

be imposed on scarce raw materials.[3] Increasing scarcities and price increases made it clear even to business that some controls were inevitable, and on February 3, 1951, Finance Minister Margaretha met with representatives of the three Chambers, the Trade Union Federation, and interested Ministries to consider appropriate measures. By February 10 the organ of the Chamber of Trade was acknowledging that world shortages made some control measures necessary, but pleaded that self-imposed business controls be tried first.[4] By February 18, the committee of interested agencies mentioned above had worked out five control bills and reached some agreement and some important disagreement on control machinery. A food control bill would make rationing possible if it proved necessary, this to be administered by the Ministries of Interior (Socialist) and Agriculture (People's Party). The second and third bills would place potential controls on industrial raw materials and on foreign trade, respectively. The fourth bill would make all rationed commodities subject to price control.

More important, there was agreement upon establishment of a new "Economic Directorate" to decide when the new rules should go into effect, coordinate the various administering agencies, and bring investment policy into harmony with the demands of the raw material situation. The chancellor would serve as chairman of the Directorate, the other members to be the vice-chancellor and the Ministers of Foreign Affairs, Interior, Social Affairs, Finance, Agriculture and Forestry, Trade, and Nationalized Industry. Unanimity would be required for all decisions. Representatives of the three Chambers and the president of the Austrian National Bank would take part, with advisory powers only, to supply necessary technical and detailed information.[5]

A major disagreement shaped up with respect to the last-named measure, however, for the People's Party insisted that all foreign trade policy questions ought to be decided in their details by the Ministry of Trade, which was, of course, dominated by the Chamber of Trade. Socialists insisted with equal vehemence that a Foreign Trade Commission on which the Chamber of Labor was represented continue to make such decisions. After months of debate in Parliament and the press, a Foreign Trade Advisory Council was substituted for the Foreign Trade Commission. The Council, on which the Chamber of Labor was represented, could, by unanimous decision, force reconsideration by the Economic Directorate of a foreign trade decision of the Minister of Trade.

[3] *Arbeiter-Zeitung*, March 30, 1951, p. 2.
[4] *Neue Wiener Tageszeitung*, February 10, 1951, p. 1.
[5] *Arbeiter-Zeitung*, February 18, 1951, p. 1.

All five bills were finally passed by the National Assembly on April 4. Representatives of organized labor were accordingly placed in a position not only to act on direct price and wage determinations, but to help shape the production, exchange, and distribution policies that might affect prices and wages in more fundamental fashion. The fact of such labor participation in broad economic policy has remained a highly controversial issue in Austrian politics.

NEGOTIATION AND PROVISIONS OF THE AGREEMENT

As has been seen, substantial wage increases were negotiated by individual unions in the winter and spring, and substantial industrial price increases were also placed in effect during this period. Neither these actions nor the hotly fought battle over labor representation on economic control bodies were sufficient in themselves to bring on another general wage-price agreement. In February, far from seeking another general agreement, Trade Union Federation President Böhm was warning that in any general agreement prices would surely rise by a higher percentage than wages because of world market price increases. He declared that the Federation must return to the old union tradition of letting each union do the best it could in its own branch of the economy; but he revealed the currently favorable union position by warning those unions which were strong or in a key position economically not to promote inflation by using all their strength in negotiations. "Discipline and economic understanding" were allegedly necessary. This position was reaffirmed several times in March and April.[6]

A new general agreement came when three additional economic changes, involving group demands other than those of labor and management, became necessary in the late spring and early summer of 1951. They concerned (1) MEC food subsidies, (2) farm prices, and (3) utility rates.

The Mission for Economic Cooperation had long been bringing pressure on the Austrian government both to reduce total MEC aid and to eliminate all use of aid for purposes other than long-range investment. In the summer of 1950 the government made commitments to the Mission to eliminate subsidies by July 1, 1951.[7]

This move in itself called for upward revision of the prices of agricultural products, but serious distortions in the farm price structure made such revision even more pressing. The ceiling price on fluid milk

---

[6] *Arbeiter-Zeitung,* February 21 (1951), pp. 1-2; March 18, p. 2; Mission for Economic Cooperation, *Monthly Labor Report,* April 24, 1951, pp. 2-3.
[7] Mission for Economic Cooperation, *Monthly Labor Report,* April 24, 1951, pp. 3-4. In the first year of Marshall aid, 1948-49, Austrian aid totalled 280 million dollars; in 1949-50, 253 million dollars; in 1950-51, 160 million dolars.

was so low that farmers found it profitable to feed a great deal of it to swine and cattle rather than ship it to the cities, and a larger proportion than usual was probably converted into more profitable milk products for sale both at home and in Germany. In consequence, milk deliveries to Vienna dropped approximately 30 per cent in the spring of 1951. The Socialist organ charged that this was a milk boycott to force an increase in the ceiling. "There is a surplus of *Schlagobers* for coffee, but no milk for babies." The People's Party organ retorted that the previous summer's drought and the dearth of foreign feed accounted for the shortage. In any case the shortage generated strong political pressure for higher milk prices and assured some action on milk in the fifth wage-price agreement. Meanwhile, the Agriculture Ministry, which had asked the Price Commission in the Interior Ministry for a higher ceiling, authorized a subsidy of 30 groschen per liter starting June 1.[8]

Confusion reigned in grain prices, too. Wheat and rye prices were so low in relation to fodder (corn and oats) prices that farmers were feeding wheat and rye to the pigs. The Chamber of Labor claimed, on the other hand, that if prices were adjusted so as fully to reflect farmer demands for increases for wheat and rye as well as those increases required to end MEC subsidies, the price level would skyrocket by 25 to 30 per cent. A compensating wage increase of this size would have hurt the export trade seriously.[9]

The pressing need for increases in electricity, gas, and railroad rates arose chiefly from a 100 per cent rise in the price of coal in Czechoslovakia and Poland, then the chief suppliers of Austrian fuel. Because it involved municipally owned and nationalized industry, the Socialists were more keenly aware of this problem than business groups.

With these developments, the Socialist-labor strategy of eschewing general agreements in favor of bargaining by individual unions was gradually supplanted by the view that a fifth agreement should be negotiated. In late April and May, the emphasis in the writings and speeches of spokesmen for this group shifted to a stress on the importance of helping pensioners and weaker unions catch up with the inevitable rise in living costs.[10] The victory in May of Socialist Candidate Theodore Koerner over his People's Party opponent in a presidential election occasioned by the death of former President Karl

---

[8] *Arbeiter-Zeitung,* June 24 (1951), April 28, March 30, and June 16; *Neue Wiener Tageszeitung,* June 6 and 8, 1951; Institut für Wirtschaftsforschung, *Monatsbericht,* April, 1951, pp. 201-202.

[9] *Arbeiterkammer Jahrbuch,* 1951, p. 380.

[10] *Arbeiter-Zeitung,* April 24 (1951), pp. 1-2; May 13, p. 1.

Renner doubtless strengthened the willingness of labor and Socialists to meet adversary economic interests on an over-all basis.

The Chamber of Trade and the People's Party leadership continued to be coy about a general agreement and to sing the virtues of "special negotiations" long after the Chamber of Labor had changed its strategy. As late as June 16, Julius Raab, president of the Chamber of Trade and newly designated chairman of the People's Party,[11] publicly took this position,[12] but shortly thereafter it became clear that only a general agreement could soothe the grievances of labor, pensioners, farmers, sufferers from various taxes, public utility administrators, landlords, and the American Mission for Economic Cooperation.

The Chamber of Trade supported abolition of all food price subsidies on the ground that economic relations are more "normal" when consumers themselves bear the burden. While supporting the principle that there be no cut in real wages (to forestall future wage demands), business opposed a general wage increase, preferring to compensate those who had lagged behind most in previous agreements and in recent collective bargaining, particularly the public employees. The Chamber vigorously fought further equalization of wages, claiming that white collar and professional employees should now get the largest raises. It supported old age insurance for the self-employed, with federal government contributions. On taxes, business groups argued strongly for a cut in the municipal trade tax, for lower income taxes, and for greater reliance on indirect excises; otherwise income would allegedly tend to be equalized and initiative destroyed. They also sought to tie a rent increase provision to their acceptance of other terms of the proposed agreement. While admitting that some utility rate rises were necessary, the Chamber of Trade favored delaying them until the fall and keeping them as small as possible. Finally, the Chamber warned that it was "unpreventable" that part of the increased business costs resulting from the agreement should be passed on in higher prices — within the limits fixed by export trade requirements. Business could not afford to take on the major burden this time.[13]

As always, the paramount labor demand was for wage increases and pension boosts sufficient to compensate fully for the increase in cost of living resulting from the new pact. To guarantee that these measures be fully realized, the Chamber of Labor and Socialist Party

---

[11] After its defeat in the presidential election an internal change in power relationships occurred in the People's Party. The influence of farmers waned and that of business increased. In consequence the former chairman, Chancellor Leopold Figl, a representative of the agriculture element, was replaced by Raab. Two years later Raab was also to succeed Figl as chancellor.

[12] *Neue Wiener Tageszeitung*, June 16, 1951, p. 1.

[13] This summary of the position of business groups regarding the fifth agreement is based upon interviews and upon editorials and reports of speeches and press releases in *Die Neue Wiener Tageszeitung*, *Die Wiener Handelkammer*, and *Das Kleine Volksblatt*.

sought a cut in the income tax for workers and an increase in the government's contribution to the pension plan. That some increase in farm prices was inevitable was acknowledged, but labor negotiators asserted that the agriculture demands were exorbitant and did not correspond to economic requirements and that farmers would do well to increase their productivity and production and to pay a greater share of taxes. Businessmen were warned that labor reserved the right to demand additional wage increases should industrial price rises occur in the months after conclusion of the pact. Because of the sharp rise in coal prices and other production costs, the Socialist–Chamber of Labor negotiators vigorously fought for an increase in public utility rates. Conceding that there was some basis for a rent increase to permit landlords to repair and maintain old houses, the labor faction nonetheless contended that rent legislation should be considered carefully by Parliament in order to assure that increases be used only for that purpose and to provide rent subsidies to prevent the increases from cutting the real wages of workers.[14]

The Communist Party opposed the pact as vigorously as it had the others, denouncing it as a "price-usurer pact," and demanding that it be submitted to a referendum in the factories before approval by the Trade Union Federation. The most vehement denunciations of the Communist position and tactic came from the Socialists and leaders of the Chamber of Labor.[15]

Because the leading participants conducted a running press debate over impasses, the course the actual negotiations took is gratifyingly more apparent to the student in the case of the fifth agreement than in the case of any of the previous ones.

Economic and statistical technicians representing the three Chambers began early in June to discuss the implications for wages, cost of living, and taxes of various price increase proposals. Consumption patterns were examined, and computations were based on various assumptions regarding the major decisions that might later be made by top officials of the Chambers and the government.

After June 20, leading officials of the Chambers, the Trade Union Federation, the People's Party, and the Socialist Party began meeting to negotiate on their respective demands. The principal stumbling block arose from the unwillingness of the labor and Socialist groups to accept the demands for sharp increases in milk and grain prices. At the same time the Chamber of Trade inveighed against the size of the proposed increases in utility rates. If all farm and utility rate demands

---

[14] The summary of the position of labor and Socialist groups is based upon interviews, editorials, and reports of speeches and press releases in the *Arbeiter-Zeitung,* and resolutions and summaries of the labor positions as published in the 1951 *Arbeiterkammer Jahrbuch.*

[15] *Arbeiter-Zeitung,* June 16 (1951), p. 2; June 19, pp. 1-2.

were granted, a compensatory wage increase in excess of 30 per cent would have been required, and all parties agreed this would be beyond the capacity of the employers to absorb and a severe shock to the economy. At this stage of the negotiations general agreement was reached upon the principle of compensatory wage increases and upon a pension boost, but business refused the labor-Socialist demand for an increase in children's allowances and in government contributions to the pension fund. As no further progress could be made at this level, the Trade Union Federation asked that the government intervene. Chancellor Figl accordingly summoned a meeting of the Economic Directorate (its first meeting since its establishment) for June 27. In that body's deliberations the most difficult issues continued to be the size of farm price increases, utility rates, government contributions to the pension plan, rent increases, and tax relief. Substantial agreement was finally achieved on all points by July 10.

A number of other bodies had now to ratify the agreement or provide for its legal effectiveness, although in every case there was virtually complete assurance that it would be accepted with little change because the chief interests involved were the same as those represented in the negotiations. The utility rates and tax changes had to be referred to Parliament, which the coalition easily controlled. Here the only discussion consisted of the expected denunciations of the agreement by the Communists, a suggestion by one member that the government consider a reduction in postal fees for newspapers, and a complaint that radio taxes were really helping the Russians because of their control of the Austrian radio.[16]

On July 13 the Price Commission in the Interior Ministry approved the new rates and prices for food, farm products, coal, gas, and electricity. Somewhat surprisingly, the Commission did reduce a few food prices below those tentatively fixed in the negotiations.

Wage rises were incorporated into a national collective agreement signed by the presidents of the Chamber of Trade and the Trade Union Federation, both of whom had been leading figures in the negotiations. The agreement included provision for a special bipartite commission to interpret the agreement before disputes reached the labor courts.[17]

On two important issues the Economic Directorate failed to reach agreement and referred them to other organizations, not only for ratification but for negotiation. With respect to the rent rise asked by the People's Party, it was agreed that Parliament would consider the question in the autumn and that an increase would be voted. Salary increases for public employees, who had failed to keep pace with other

---

[16] *Neue Wiener Tageszeitung,* July 13, 1951, p. 1.
[17] *Neue Wiener Tageszeitung,* July 18, 1951, pp. 1, 8.

workers, were negotiated between the union representing these workers and the Minister of Finance, and an agreement was reached on July 25.

The American labor attaché in Vienna summed up the compromise character of the fifth agreement by reporting that " . . . no economic sector received full satisfaction of its demands, . . . all sectors made some sacrifices and . . . no basic problems were totally solved." This was clearly true of the most difficult issue, farm and food prices. Price increases on milk (from 1 schilling per liter to 1.40), wheat, corn, rye, and their products and on margarine and vegetable shortening were substantially lower than those first asked by the Chamber of Agriculture. The doubling of coal costs allowed less leeway for compromising the Socialist demands for increases in postage, telephone rates, gas, electricity, and railroad fares.

When these increases were computed on the basis of a revised consumption pattern, it was estimated they would mean a cost of living increase of 47 schillings a month for a child and 127 schillings for two adults. To compensate, a series of wage and tax measures was adopted. Manual workers were granted a monthly boost of 10 per cent or 140 schillings, whichever was greater, white collar workers 12 per cent or 140 schillings. The children's allowance rose from 60 to 105 schillings per month. The income tax was revised so as to exempt the new wage increases from taxation, partly through an increase in tax-free social insurance contributions. Depending on previous salary and number of dependents, these changes meant net income rises ranging from 14.6 per cent to 29.4 per cent.

Pensions advanced 10 per cent plus 80 schillings for single persons and 125 schillings for those with dependents, with advance provision for a further increase when the new rent schedules should become effective. A new clause suspended or reduced pension payments if earnings should reach specified maxima. Both unemployment insurance and the relief payments made after exhaustion of insurance benefits were increased by the same formula as pensions.

A number of tax changes besides that in the income tax were important for business. The employer contribution to the children's allowance fund, formerly 3 per cent of payrolls, was now fixed at 6 per cent. The turnover tax was increased from .85 per cent to 1.7 per cent on wholesale sales and from 3.4 to 5 per cent on retail sales. Excises on vehicles, oil, and transportation were increased. Business benefited, however, from a cut in the municipal trade tax. Socialists were unhappy about this move because they believed it would seriously hurt the Socialist-governed municipalities in industrial areas, and some even declared this was one of the People's Party's intentions. Socialists announced they would vote for it in Parliament only on the assumption the municipalities would later be compensated.[18]

Agreement on the principle of a rent increase and a compensatory housing subsidy was achieved in the negotiations in the Economic Directorate, but the details were left for Parliamentary decision. This was the first important item of business when Parliament convened in September, 1951. The People's Party's case for an increase was a strong one and was not seriously challenged. Rents on old houses had been frozen since the first world war[19] and had, in fact, been reduced by one third at the time of the Anschluss in 1938. Other prices had increased seven- to ten-fold in the same period of years. The phenomenally low rents had meant that repairs and improvements to old houses were rare. Virtually the only new house construction was of municipal apartment buildings.

The controversies centered around the financing of the compensatory subsidy and restrictions upon the uses to which rent increases could be put. The People's Party took the position that subsidies should be paid out of the existing social insurance fund, but Socialists succeeded in securing an increase of .75 per cent in employers' social insurance contributions to cover the new 30 schilling subsidy. Socialists also made it a condition of their acceptance of the rent increase that landlords be permitted to use the additional income only to make repairs and improvements, and this too was ultimately accepted.[20]

The parties themselves and the Austrian Institute of Economic Research were in substantial agreement in their respective discussions of the relative sacrifice involved in the fifth agreement. Pensioners and public employees bettered their real wages and thus improved their relative position, as did farmers. Wage earners as a whole maintained their position and probably improved it, at least until secondary price increases set in. Business took on additional burdens, although it was assumed and hoped that these would be paid out of the profits made possible by rising production and productivity and by price increases since the last agreement. Export business was relatively well off compared to firms producing for the domestic market, for the latter were subjected not only to increased production costs but to a market characterized by severely limited purchasing power.[21]

---

[18] Institut für Wirtschaftsforschung, "Das Fünfte Lohn-Preis Abkommen," in *Monatsbericht*, August, 1951, p. 7; *Arbeiter-Zeitung*, July 19 (1951), p. 2; July 21, p. 2.

[19] Increases were possible only if approved by a court or rent commission on application of the landlord and one half the tenants.

[20] Cf. *#440 der Beilagen zu den Stenographisches Protokoll des Nationalrates*, "Bericht und Antrag des Justizausschusses;" *Neue Wiener Tageszeitung*, September 14 (1951), p. 1, September 19, p. 1, September 22, pp. 1-2; *Arbeiter-Zeitung*, September 19 (1951), p. 1, September 20, p. 1.

[21] Institut für Wirtschaftsforschung, "Das Fünfte Lohn-Preis Abkommen," in *Monatsbericht*, August, 1951; *Arbeiter-Zeitung*, July 18, 1951, pp. 1-2; *Neue Wiener Tageszeitung*, September 2, 1951, p. 2.

The price increases of the fifth agreement shocked Austrian consumers to a degree still easily discernible when the writer visited the country more than a year later. But the wage increases preceding and incorporated in the pact, the careful preparation of worker opinion, and public willingness to accept the fact that the Korean War inevitably meant economic instability for Austria prevented a repetition of the Communist disturbances that had followed the announcement of the terms of the fourth agreement.

Almost immediately after the readjustments called for in the pact had been instituted, the usual secondary price increases began to appear and in such marked form that all parties became alarmed at the possibility that the wage-price spiral was continuing without check. An immediate consequence of the concern was an agreement in September, 1951, by representatives of the three Chambers, the Trade Union Federation, and the Association of Austrian Industrialists on a program of restraint in wage demands in return for voluntary price cuts. A widely publicized campaign for the voluntary cuts continued through the fall and early winter and brought reductions of 3 to 5 per cent on some consumer items, though the "voluntary" aspect was doubtless abetted by a falling off in consumer demand and sales and an increase of 1.5 per cent in the interest rate in November.[22]

Compared to its fluctuations in the first six postwar years, the Austrian cost of living index remained fairly stable following the fifth agreement. Changes were slight in 1952, 1953, and in 1954 to the present writing.

---

[22] Cf. Institut für Wirtschaftsforschung, *Monatsberichte* for the final months of 1951.

CHAPTER 7 Summary and Conclusions

The record of events chronicled here provides some clues as to the dynamics of interaction between public policy and private economic activity. Occasionally the clues may be multiplied by comparison or contrast with experience elsewhere in which some of the conditions were different.

Central to an understanding of this interaction in Austria is recognition that the unique feature of the Austrian political and economic scene during the years under consideration was the ability of virtually every economic group interest to checkmate every other, coupled with the ability of the two broad political alignments to checkmate each other. Both labor and farm groups could strike and thereby seriously threaten the recovery program and directly injure the other economic groupings. Business could accomplish the same purpose by raising industrial prices and expanding credit. Dismal living standards and the widespread interest in economic recovery made such injuries really hurt. During the first seven postwar years each of these tactics was utilized enough to make its reality and its ominous effects clear to the others. On the political scene, the People's Party and the Socialists were evenly enough matched that either could block legislative and executive programs. The fact that the two major political parties were so close in voting support also conferred extraordinary bargaining power on usually defenseless unorganized groups like the pensioners, for their support at the polls might mean the difference between defeat and victory.

In group terms, this set of conditions meant that each economic group shared the interests of all the others, for to ignore them was to invite self-injury. The structure of balance of group strength is best highlighted by contrasting it with conditions at other times and places which serve as rough "control" situations. In the twenties and early 1930's the Austrian Socialists usually polled a higher vote than any other party, but a rightist coalition was able to keep them out of the government and thus prevent their exercising any great bargaining power on political decisions. In 1934 the Dollfuss regime utilized the Fascist home guard, the "Heimwehr," the regular army, and a Party guard to suppress the Socialist Party and trade unions and to prevent the workers from exercising collective economic power. These measures were possible in 1934 because the rightist group controlled the police and military forces and no equivalent force existed elsewhere to prevent their use.[1] In the postwar period Austria had no army, and the police force was not available for use by any political faction. Fresh and poignant memories of the 1934 violence, which had been followed shortly by Nazi aggression, largely precluded another rightist coalition as a political possibility,[2] and the Western occupation powers did not conceal their aversion for abandonment of the Socialist–People's Party coalition. Resort to force on the 1934 pattern would probably have brought forceful intervention by the four occupying powers.

There was, then, no possibility of ignoring the bargaining weapons of any economic or political group. Stalemate was a far more probable outcome than was domination by any one group. By the same token, however, such domination was a possibility if any of the following key changes should occur: (1) a marked improvement in production and living standards, which would significantly reduce the efficacy of the economic weapons of a strike or rise in prices; (2) restoration of a politically oriented army or police force; (3) withdrawal of the occupying powers.

ECONOMIC TRENDS AND POLICY CHANGE

Given this political setting, were there consistent relationships between economic trends and public policy? The record shows some strikingly consistent ones although they cannot be stated in quantitative terms on the basis of this limited experience.[3] Each of the general agreements except the third occurred when farm income lagged substantially behind that of other economic sectors and threatened to lag even more unless policy changes intervened. On each occasion negotiators for the other economic groups admitted that the Chamber of Agriculture's claims were in some measure justified and that failure to remedy the maladjustment would impede economic recovery. Because farm prices were controlled, the only possible remedial measures were authorization for farm price increases or roll-backs in industrial prices and wages, with the latter alternative obviously the more burdensome and difficult for all concerned. Although labor groups joined in this

---

[1] Although more farsighted Christian Socialist leaders than Dollfuss and Schuschnigg might have easily foreseen that suppression of the Socialists and unions rendered Austria defenseless against an invasion by Hitler.

[2] Rumors of the possibility during the cabinet crisis of February, 1953, brought prompt and vehement opposition in coffee house conversation and in the press.

[3] If accurate indexes of all economic trends, including black market prices and industrial profits were available, a statement in arithmetic terms would probably be possible. It may be equally or more persuasive, however, to rely upon general agreement among adversary economic groups that at the time of a particular policy change a stated group was at a disadvantage compared to the others.

estimate, they were consistently less willing to concur in the full agricultural demands than were business groups, who were allied to the farmers in the People's Party. It may therefore be said that, given existing political conditions, a public policy change of increased farm prices occurred when (1) the farmers' share of the national product lagged proportionately behind that of other groups; (2) continuation of existing price policy would predictably perpetuate or aggravate the lag; and (3) these conditions and their adverse effect on economic recovery were recognized by the other economic sectors. How large a price increase was granted depended at least in part upon the extent to which each sector would be injured by the farm price maladjustment.

Changes in wage policy are explainable by a similar analysis. Each time a farm price readjustment was necessary the workers' share of the national product would predictably have been reduced substantially in the absence of concomitant remedial policy changes — with predictable dire consequences for productivity, production, and purchasing power, i.e., for businessmen and farmers. Hence it was precisely at these times that general wage increases were granted. The fact that the lowest paid and most weakly organized workers consistently secured the fattest increases in the agreements is further evidence for the hypothesis here suggested.[4]

How *large* a wage increase labor was able to get through governmental action is similarly related to the extent of its lag behind other claimants on the national product. Both in Austrian and in recent American experience with wage stabilization programs, the formulas for wage increases have been more generous to labor when this lag was greater. In Austria industrial prices were not controlled at all. Given organized labor's ability to impose economic and political sanctions, labor was able to insist successfully on the policy of wage increases sufficient to compensate for the price increases. In the American stabilization program of 1950-51, labor was able to do the same once it was clear that price control was a fiction. During World War II, however, the Little Steel Formula and other policies broke the tie between wages and living costs, and this is the one instance in which there was a fairly effective price control program. The absence of price control means a heavy disproportionate sacrifice by labor and therefore a strong demand for compensatory wage increases. If labor is able to back up the

---

[4] The intimate relevance of the basic condition stated above is obvious. Without the ability of strong unions to strike and the ability of all labor to exercise formidable political strength through its votes and inside the Socialist Party, the dire consequences for businessmen and farmers might have been avoided and the general wage increases not granted, despite grievous cuts in the workers' real income. Nothing in the history of early nineteenth century British labor or, indeed, of medieval vassalage contradicts the inference that the worker group without either economic or political recourse can do little to increase its share of the national product.

demand with political or economic sanctions, as it was able to do both in Austria and in the 1950-51 American program, it is likely to achieve compensatory increases as a policy.

Pension policy changes afford an instructive supplement to the hypothesis regarding the necessary conditions for raising the wages of the lowest paid workers. Pensions were usually increased in the wage-price agreements by a percentage equal to the anticipated increase in living costs or by a slightly higher amount. Pensioners had no formal organization and no obvious technique for bringing pressure upon other groups except as they constituted a minor segment of the Trade Union Federation and the Socialist Party. Yet the claim of this group to pension increases was consistently brought to the attention of the wage-price negotiators and was consistently granted without controversy. It was a factor apparently regarded as compelling by all groups participating in the policy decisions. The influence of this group is explicable on the hypothesis that no other group was willing to risk the predictable political odium that would follow upon advocacy of reducing still further the already miserable estate of the Austrian pensioner — a sensitivity which many Austrians regarded as enhanced by the close tie of the Chambers to the leading political parties. This phenomenon throws added light on the ability of low-wage workers to get relief in the agreements, and strongly suggests that such relief would have been forthcoming regardless of the tie of these workers to strong or weak unions. On this hypothesis it is also predictable that pensioners will be granted increases at any time a sudden and substantial planned rise in living costs occurs or periodically as gradual increases cumulate.

Tax changes are best understood in terms of the economic benefits and sacrifices to the respective groups flowing from governmental budget policy. Just as each of the wage-price agreements involved an additional burden for business in order to bring its share of the national product in line with that of competing groups, so tax policy reflected the same phenomenon. In each agreement changes in the income tax structure or in social security contributions meant additional business financial burdens, at least until industrial price increases again gave business an advantage. The only important exception was the cut in the municipal trade tax after the fifth agreement, and other tax increases in this agreement followed the customary pattern of new burdens for business. Although Chamber of Trade negotiators complained in public about most of these tax burdens, they accepted them, for business had a calculable need on these occasions to sufficiently appease farm, labor, and pensioner demands to permit economic recovery to continue without political or economic upheavals. The problem that gave rise to the third agreement, while on its face a budgetary deficit, is understood better as a need for meeting inescapable commitments for occupation costs and pensions. This was supplemented by a desire to prevent the farm price crisis that would predictably arise if ECA aid were cut without some domestic provision for partial subsidies and for the transfer of part of the new burden to labor and business.

ORGANIZATION AND POLICY CHANGE

It has already been suggested that government is group activity viewed as comprehensive organization, as distinguished from viewing it as social trends, individual activity, or primary groups. While the "transaction" to be studied is the same in all cases, the suggested perspective means relatively more emphasis on some aspects and less on others. The observer is thereby enabled to study some things he cannot see at all from other perspectives. Several phases of the rather unusual Austrian organizational arrangement suggest propositions about the relation of organization to policy change, especially when compared with alternative organizational arrangements in the United States. In reviewing this material it should be kept in mind that "organization," "interests," and "trends" are to be defined only in terms of each other. They are not discrete "factors" which interact with each other.

The condition that each of the economic groupings could wield formidable sanctions over the others by delaying economic recovery was reflected organizationally in their formal membership on the Economic Commission and other bodies that negotiated the general agreements. Review of the occasions on which the United States has resorted to tripartitism or bipartitism indicates that here too it has occurred whenever labor or management organizations were in a position to prevent the success of a program by resort to independent action. This has been true of the long succession of permanent and *ad hoc* tripartite bodies set up to mediate and arbitrate labor disputes on the railroads, and it is true of the bipartite National Railroad Adjustment Board today. The ultimate explanation for tripartitism on the War Labor Board and Wage Stabilization Board was that it reflected organizationally the judgment that no particular compromise between a tight wage freeze and full satisfaction of higher wage demands was workable without a fairly high degree of voluntary compliance.

In each case, therefore, partisan representation on the government agency offered both a convenient forum for resolving group conflicts and an opportunity for either side to veto wholly unacceptable policies by walking out. By withdrawing from the Economic Commission which negotiated the Austrian wage-price agreements, any one of the three Chambers could have scuttled the Commission and the agreement, just as American labor could and did scuttle the National Defense Mediation Board in 1941 and force reorganization and policy changes in the Wage Stabilization Board in 1951 by withdrawing from these bodies. Experience with formal representation of private groups on public bodies suggests two conclusions then: (1) It occurs when the private groups are able to sabotage a governmental program by private action.[5] (2) It effectively limits the range of possible policy decisions available to the agency in question. Such influence is essentially the same as that wielded by voting constituents of an elected official or by legal superiors of a governmental unit, and may accordingly be conveniently designated "constituent" power. The Austrian Chambers and Trade Union Federation wielded such constituent power not only in the Economic Commission, but also in the coalition cabinet and in Parliament as well in proportion as the two major political parties were identified with the respective economic sectors.

Another proposition that has been suggested in other studies[6] gains confirmation from this one — that a group's strength in any organizational unit is lessened as the unit's jurisdiction is widened to include more group interests. From late 1945 to the first agreement in September, 1947, wages, agricultural prices, and industrial prices were "controlled" by separate agencies, each of which responded sensitively to the strong interests in higher wages, farm income, and profits, respectively, with little heed for the unstabilizing effect of its decisions on the others. This very fact created a strong interest in a more comprehensive organization which would be forced to consider the effects of each policy on all others under its jurisdiction.

The result clearly was far more restraint than had been in evidence prior to the first agreement. In the general agreements, farmers accepted prices which had not risen as much relative to 1937 levels as either industrial prices or wages and also reluctantly accepted continuing farm price subsidies, although the Agriculture Ministry, with jurisdiction only over farm problems, favored much higher farm prices and higher consumer prices for food in place of subsidies. Organized labor repeatedly sought to keep prices down rather than demand wage

---

[5] In American experience with administration of labor law the converse of this proposition has also been true; *viz.*, that labor and management organizations have not been given formal representation, but only advisory status, on those programs which they were not in a position to sabotage by private action. Examples are NRA, the industry committees under the 1938 Fair Labor Standards Act, and advisory committees under various state minimum wage laws.

[6] Murray Edelman, "Governmental Organization and Public Policy," *Public Administration Review*, Autumn, 1952, pp. 276-283.

boosts, and in the negotiations asked only for increases sufficient to compensate for living costs — this, despite the fact that many unions could have done better by bringing economic pressure against the employers in their own industries.[7] Business bore the chief financial burden of each of the agreements, in this manner compensating negatively for industrial price rises between agreements. But the Ministry of Trade, with narrow jurisdiction only over business groups, sought consistently for more business influence and favored smaller wage increases than those actually granted. All the parties whose cooperation was necessary to the agreements sanctioned the policy of according larger increases to workers with low incomes, and all agreed to accord compensatory increases to pensioners and the unorganized, even though these groups had no direct representation.

In short, the general negotiations inevitably meant that there would be comprehensive and detailed awareness of the needs and the weapons of every other claimant on the national product. Common awareness of the needs of each group and also of the problems likely to be created by failure to satisfy these needs was further enhanced by the circumstance that each of the economic Chambers employed competent economists and statisticians and maintained impressive libraries and statistical records. In these respects they were better equipped than the government Ministries and far better equipped than Parliament. These facilities plus the comprehensive jurisdiction of the Economic Committee that negotiated the general agreements meant that in a very significant sense the interests of each group were spread to the other groups and each demand was thereby compromised to take account of others.

These propositions are useful in explaining the absence of controls over industrial prices, credit, and interim wage negotiations in postwar Austria. These matters differed from those covered in the general negotiations in two respects. First, there were strong groups within both the labor and the management organizations who opposed controls so that the interest in controlling these matters in the general negotiations was relatively weak. Second, it would have been administratively difficult to carry out any control policy, for both sides supported the older, more narrowly drawn control agencies. Industrial prices especially had long been so thoroughly regulated by the Chamber of Trade that the other economic groups lacked both the bargaining power to get a voice in the matter and the means to effectuate any general policy that might have been adopted. Socialist concern was further weakened by the fact that some of the most important industry

---

[7] Spokesmen for business as well as labor groups agreed that most unions could have won larger immediate gains by direct bargaining.

was nationalized. Both the Socialists and the People's Party had large investments in the banks and were not, therefore, easy to arouse about the need for credit control.[8] Productivity gains and relatively favorable profits weakened the resistance of some of the larger industries to strong union pressure for interim wage increases. Also relevant to an explanation of these uncontrolled practices was the fact that their differential impact on the various economic groupings was not easily understood or the subject of general agreement even among professional economists. Consequently support for a control policy was more difficult to arouse. In short, interest in control of these matters was relatively weak because of adversary factions within both labor and management, conflicting or vague information about their impact, and significant administrative difficulties.

Increases in industrial prices, credit, or the earnings of strongly organized workers were, in fact, controlled to a significant degree by conflicting groups within the private organizations responsible for their administration. Even without government controls, industry could not raise industrial prices indefinitely because of the predictable disadvantages such a course would have on export trade, foreign exchange, taxes, economic recovery (in short, on various business groups), and on the inclination of farmers and labor to push for compensating concessions. Interim wage increases were held in bounds by some of these same considerations plus the predictable disadvantages of larger increases on employment and living costs (in short, on various labor groups).

Still another organizational facet worth brief consideration is the role of "public members" in the American wage stabilization programs and their absence in Austria. From the point of view of group accommodation, public members served two functions. They mediated, or arbitrated, between adversary labor and management groups, and they represented such demands as labor and management had in common to higher levels of the governmental hierarchy.[9] So far as the first of these functions is concerned, the public members had little impact upon policy, for on such issues as union security and the relation of wages to prices (or lack thereof), on which unions and management had plainly adversary objectives, a compromise solution acceptable to both sides was essential. The public members probably did little more than enable the partisan members to indulge in politically useful face-

---

[8] Of the three nationalized banks, the largest, the Credit-Anstalt, was under People's Party control, and the next largest, the Länderbank, under Socialist control. Although economists in the Chamber of Labor felt rather strongly that credit should have been controlled, one of them told the writer that it had been impossible to flout those Socialist officials interested in existing banking arrangements.

[9] For a more detailed discussion of these functions of the public members, see Edelman, *op. cit.*

saving through the device of dissenting for the record. In Austria compromise results on adversary issues were arrived at by direct negotiation. Although the chancellor and cabinet members sometimes participated in the final stages, their tie to political parties and sometimes to economic Chambers prevented their serving the same function as the American public members. It would, in fact, be remarkably difficult to find any expert in Austria capable of posing as a neutral, even among the college faculty groups favored for this ceremonial role in America. The American public members unquestionably did affect policy when they represented joint labor-management demands at higher governmental levels, for such direct organizational representation at higher levels is a distinct advantage for any group. In Austria, however, this function also was superfluous, for each of the economic groups was itself directly represented in the cabinet as well as in the Economic Commission. It may therefore be suggested that so far as high level representation of accommodated labor-management aims are concerned, the American device of public members served somewhat the same purpose as the Austrian institution of a coalition government with intimate ties to business and labor organizations.

What has been said clarifies somewhat the bearing of factional differences within the political parties, the Chambers, and the unions upon the intensity of group demands and policy changes. An impressive, though incomplete, list of factional differences was cited at the beginning of this paper. The study indicates that one consequence of such internal differences has been that certain practices have not been controlled by general agreement at all. Cases in point are industrial price setting, credit policy, and collective bargaining on wages between general agreements. In the case of these practices, factional differences cut through the organizations that acted as adversaries in the general wage-price negotiations. Within each organization, a significant faction favored retention of existing practices rather than negotiation in the agreements. Factional differences served, moreover, to keep unilateral control of these practices by one of the organizations or bilateral negotiation between two of them within bounds acceptable to nonparticipating organizations. In the case of industrial prices the Chamber of Trade made most of the decisions. In the case of credit policy, it was the banks and the Finance Ministry. In the case of collective bargaining, it was a specific industrial union and the Chamber of Trade or some subdivision of the Chamber. In each instance, built-in adversary interests kept policies reasonably moderate.

But this applies to only a few of the economic policies. With respect to most of them, factional differences did not prevent each of the

Chambers, the political parties, and the Trade Union Federation from formulating a position acceptable enough to their respective members that no faction seceded (except for secession of some Communists from unions). The policy position would doubtless have been different in each set of economic circumstances if the internal factional pattern had been different. If, for example, banking interests had constituted a larger and more powerful faction within the Chamber of Trade, the Chamber's opposition to the fiscal reform law of December, 1947, would certainly have been stronger and the resulting legislation probably less drastic. Regardless of the relative strength of the various factions, however, the growing oversupply of currency tended to move all factions in the direction of supporting some kind of fiscal reform, though with divergencies in zeal. Similarly, the periodic recurrence of farm price crises created some demand in all factions for a farm price increase. A different factional pattern would have meant a different intensity and consequently a larger or smaller increase than those actually granted.

SUMMARY OF THE CONCEPTUAL MODEL

Although it is necessary in setting down these observations to refer to the correlation of stated policies with particular trends, the relationships suggested operate only in the total environment described, and generalization must therefore be understood to be rigorously qualified by the condition that the political, organizational, and economic conditions are those that prevailed in Austria. In applying such transactional analysis to other times and places, variations in any of these relevant conditions may mean some variation in all the others, though the model suggested by the Austrian experience may help explain what kind of variation in the others.

For this study it seems useful to regard the existing constituent powers of various organizations as the context within which the creation and interplay of group interests occurs. This conceptual framework is useful only because, for the data of this study and probably for most others, the constituency arrangements are more continuous (that is, more strongly supported) than the groups involved in the policies under review. By constituency is meant a group able to weaken or abolish public organizations if their policies are unacceptable.

The arrangement of constituent powers in postwar Austria may be defined as follows. Each of the two broad political alignments was able to prevent the other from taking unilateral executive or legislative action, even on relatively detailed matters. Stalemates between these alignments could not be broken by the forceful suppression of either because of their virtual equality of numbers, absence of an army or political police, and the presence of foreign troops.[10] Agriculture, labor, and business groups, when not internally divided on an issue, were each able to checkmate the others by economic tactics, a circumstance promoted by the extremely low living standard, the fact that productive facilities were inadequate, and the high degree to which each economic sector was organized.

Assuming these conditions, it is possible to generalize that whenever the share of one of the claimants on the national product, usually agriculture, shrank substantially in relation to the shares of the other major claimants, general negotiations were instituted to readjust the shares so as to prevent immediate injury to the claimants in question and long-run injury to other groups.[11] An external event usually precipitated most of the shrinkage of one of the claimants' shares, although the relatively uncontrolled economic decisions on industrial prices and credit were also responsible for gradual shrinkage. The external events in question were the economic consequences of the Second World War, the cuts in Marshall aid, and the Korean War with its aftermath of rising world market prices and goods shortages. These events were not subject to Austrian control, but they had the effect of raising food prices and, in the case of the third agreement, of precipitating a severe budgetary crisis. The agreements invariably rescued the farmers from the baneful effects of these trends and simultaneously re-established the relative positions of other groups unable to help themselves through any of the uncontrolled institutions, *viz.*, pensioners and unorganized or weakly organized workers.

From the perspective of organization, the study confirms the hypothesis that a group is weakened in an organizational unit of government in the degree that the unit's jurisdiction is widened to include concern for other groups, especially if the groups favoring the alternative objectives are organized and able to wield economic or political sanctions.

Formal representation of private groups in a government agency occurs when their cooperation is necessary to the execution of the

---

[10] It is presumably the basic stability, not the particular reasons for it, that matters. In another country a similar stability buttressed upon different sanctions might have similar implications for policy formation.

[11] An important implicit condition here is that the long-run implications and dangers were fairly clear, even though there was considerable difference in emphasis regarding them as between different groups. Both business and labor groups admitted, for example, that continuation of low and distorted farm prices would mean less food production and inefficient distribution and would have undesirable effects on the entire population, including themselves. With respect to policies in other contexts there might be a significant divergence among rival groups in economic theory, which might mean a different correlation between policy changes and economic trends than agreement in theory would produce. Put another way, academic theory — in military tactics, soil conservation, economics, or other fields in which government acts — has political implications not only because of what the theory is but also because of the degree of its acceptance.

agency's program. Such representation enables the group in question to limit the range of agency sensitivity to other group interests within its jurisdiction.

In any government which pretends to operate in accordance with the consent of the governed, there must be provision for ascertaining the needs of all groups and the impact of existing and proposed policies upon them. This is an information-gathering and evaluating function, and its adequacy depends upon the sufficiency of channels of communication and the access of groups to government agencies.[12] Most persons, however, have no opinion on policies that affect them and are not likely to voice their needs unless and until conditions arise that make the impact of a particular policy immediately important to them. Inflexible enforcement of mortgage contracts is not important to debtors in prosperous times, but may mean forceful prevention of sheriffs' sales in time of depression. Loose price controls become the object of active hostility from consumers only when prices begin to soar or income to fall. All democratic governments consequently need a device whereby groups can try to veto or actually veto policies that seriously hurt them, i.e., exercise a constituent function.

One way of defining the difference between the Austrian system and more customary arrangements is to point out the identity in Austria of organizations for gathering data and the constituent organizations. The Chambers and the Trade Union Federation were both. In the United States it is common for unions, trade associations, and other "private" organizations to make their needs and wishes known to legislative and administrative bodies. Only rarely, however, is any measure of constituent authority delegated to them rather than to voters in various geographical districts or to legal superiors. Retention of constituent powers by the latter groups is a method of assuring that all groups with common interests, organized or not, can veto policies if they are large enough and seriously enough affected.

Combination of the two functions in the Austrian fashion carries with it the grave danger that some group interest will be without access and unheard and consequently suppressed or oppressed — the essence of Fascism and tryanny. This has not in fact happened because the organizations which negotiated the agreements did not leave any significant groups out of consideration. That they did not is at least partly explicable by the fact that the major political parties were not entirely controlled by the Chambers and the opposition parties not at all so controlled.

When conditions are such that the groups involved in a program

---

[12] The concept of "access" and this entire phenomenon are analyzed in David Truman, *The Governmental Process* (New York: Knopf, 1951).

would be hurt, even by relatively slight changes in policy, combination of the two functions has the advantage that the formulation of policy is automatically kept within bounds acceptable to the groups concerned before any injury occurs. Conditions in Austria were of this kind. It is obvious, however, that continuation of this arrangement into more "normal" conditions would bring with it the danger of denying access to groups which rely only on geographical representation and not on functional representation for access.

The Austrian experience has been dramatic. In a sense it has been unique. More transactional studies of policy formation over a sufficiently long time period and dealing with sufficiently varied conditions may suggest precise definitions of the unique and the comparable and possibly produce cumulative knowledge of social and political process.

TABLE 1. Cost of Living Index, Vienna[a]

(APRIL, 1945 = 100)

YEAR	MONTH	ALL ITEMS	FOOD
1938	April	78.5	78.7
1945	April	100.0	100.0
1946	April	113.4	112.6
	October	134.9	140.6
	December	143.7	148.4
1947	January	145.4	150.1
	April	168.7	158.2
	July	260.5	275.3
	October	350.2	333.9
	December	357.0	343.9
1948	January	359.6	346.9
	April	364.3	355.3
	July	358.2	251.2
	October	423.0	464.5
	December	432.7	482.6
1949	January	435.1	486.8
	April	427.8	480.1
	July	509.1	589.8
	October	521.4	568.3
	December	560.0	630.9
1950	January	555.6	621.9
	April	524.2	557.3
	July	535.6	572.2
	October	577.9	612.8
	December	598.3	642.2
1951	January	611.3	645.7
	April	624.8	629.3
	July	716.2	767.6
	October	784.7	803.3
	December	832.0	870.2

[a] Based upon statistics published by the Austrian Institute of Economic Research.

TABLE 2. Ratio of Black Market to Official Prices, Vienna[a]

(OFFICIAL PRICES = 1)

YEAR	MONTH	FOOD	LUXURY FOOD ITEMS
1945	August	255.2	122.1
1946	(average)	107.2	23.4
	April	168.0	21.0
	July	105.0	9.0
	October	45.0	4.0
	December	43.0	4.0
1947	(average)	27.2	3.1
	January	39.4	4.0
	April	35.4	3.6
	May	34.2	3.2
	June	31.8	3.7
	July	18.4	2.8
	August	18.6	2.7
	September	18.1	2.9
	October	18.2	2.9
	December	23.3	2.9
1948	January	12.7	2.7
	February	10.1	2.3
	March	9.7	2.5
	April	7.5	2.9
	May	5.7	2.4
	June	5.6	2.1

[a] Prices from mid-month for food weighted according to peacetime consumption pattern. 1938 schilling = 1948 schilling. Based upon statistics published by the Austrian Institute of Economic Research.

TABLE 3. Index of Hourly Earnings, Vienna[a]

(APRIL, 1945 = 100)

YEAR	MONTH	TOTAL	SKILLED	UNSKILLED	FEMALE
1946	April	114.7	113.2	138.3	98.8
	July	129.4	123.6	147.1	124.8
	October	137.6	131.8	150.7	136.7
	December	158.6	151.5	198.0	139.5
1947	January	163.8	151.7	195.1	158.9
	April	174.1	160.1	204.6	173.1
	July	209.5	191.5	246.7	209.3
	October	305.1	270.7	365.1	313.7
	December	305.1	270.7	365.1	313.7
1948	January	305.1	270.7	365.1	313.7
	April	305.1	270.7	365.1	313.7
	July	307.9	273.2	368.9	316.0
	October	374.8	329.5	447.4	391.1
	December	376.5	330.7	449.7	393.1
1949	January	376.5	330.7	449.7	393.1
	April	376.5	330.7	449.7	393.1
	July	418.3	363.2	494.7	447.2
	October	418.3	363.2	494.7	447.2
	December	418.3	363.2	494.7	447.2
1950	January	422.0	366.8	449.1	450.4
	April	423.2	369.3	499.1	450.4
	July	436.5	381.7	531.8	450.4
	October	514.3	445.2	620.2	542.5
	December	514.3	445.2	620.2	542.5
1951	January	526.1	458.3	622.5	559.7
	April	566.5	495.4	670.2	599.7
	July	705.7	608.1	826.8	767.5
	October	705.6	608.8	826.4	766.4
	December	723.8	623.4	847.5	788.0

[a] Calculated on the basis of average hourly wages in industry and trade for a 48-hour week for a married person with two children, after deduction of taxes, social insurance, and union dues. Based upon statistics published in the *Monthly Reports* of the Austrian Institute of Economic Research. Beginning with January, 1950, children's allowances are taken into account.

TABLE 4. Index of Net Income, Vienna[a]

(AUGUST, 1938 = 100)

YEAR	MONTH	TOTAL	SKILLED	UNSKILLED	FEMALE
1946	April	80.2	81.9	68.1	86.9
1947	January	106.9	103.7	116.1	104.8
	April	120.3	117.7	123.5	121.8
	July	164.1	153.6	166.8	178.6
	October	250.9	225.3	250.5	291.7
	December	258.1	229.1	254.6	306.9
1948	January	241.1	214.2	229.8	292.6
	April	265.8	237.8	263.0	312.5
	July	273.9	247.0	274.2	316.4
	October	316.6	284.4	307.9	374.3
	December	329.7	285.1	315.7	411.7
1949	January	324.8	283.4	310.8	401.2
	April	346.1	309.3	336.8	411.7
	July	384.5	347.8	365.2	467.2
	October	322.3	345.9	383.6	472.8
	December	403.2	356.4	379.7	495.7
1950	January	378.0	334.8	352.0	466.4
	April	398.6	344.2	381.8	497.9
	July	402.9	352.4	396.3	488.1
	October	501.7	441.6	485.3	609.5
	December	509.1	448.4	465.5	638.8
1951	January	484.9	426.1	450.2	605.1
	April	513.8	445.3	473.9	653.2
	July	573.8	501.3	540.7	714.5
	October	673.2	582.2	627.6	852.6

[a] For a married person with two children. Based upon statistics published in the *Monthly Reports* of the Austrian Institute of Economic Research. After October, 1948, children's allowances are taken into account. After June, 1947, a broader base was employed and figures are therefore not directly comparable with previous ones.

BIBLIOGRAPHY

Adamovich, Ludwig. *Grundriss des Österreichischen Verfassungsrechtes.* Vienna: 1947.

Austria — A Graphic Survey. Vienna: Office of the U. S. High Commissioner, 1952.

Gulick, Charles A. *Austria from Habsburg to Hitler.* Berkeley: University of California, 1948.

Jahrbuch. Vienna: Vienna Chamber of Labor, annual.

Johnstone, Harry. *The Restraint of Competition in the Austrian Economy.* Vienna: Office of the U. S. High Commissioner, 1951.

Kravis, Irving B. "Prices and Wages in the Austrian Economy, 1938-47," *Monthly Labor Review,* January, 1948, pp. 20-27.

MacDonald, Mary. *The Republic of Austria.* London: Oxford, 1946.

Monatsberichte des Österreichischen Institutes für Wirtschaftsforschung. Vienna: Austrian Institute of Economic Research, monthly.

Staribacher, Josef. "Ziele und Möglichkeiten der behördlichen Preisbildung und die Preisbildung in Österreich seit 1945." Unpublished Ph.D. dissertation, Vienna, 1950.

Stupperger, Leopold. "Die Entwicklung der Arbeiterkammern in Österreich." Unpublished Ph.D. dissertation, Vienna, 1949.

Index

Agricultural interests, 9, 11, 38, 47, 67; *see also* Chamber of Agriculture; Farmers; People's party.

Agricultural prices, 10, 24, 26, 27, 31, 36, 49, 53, 58, 62, 66; quotas, 24; income, 25

Agriculture and Forestry, Minister of, 12, 19, 24, 48, 50, 62

Allied military authorities, 19, 30, 40, 58

America, comparisons with, 9, 11, 12, 37, 40, 43, 54, 59, 60, 61, 62, 64, 67, 68; *see* Allied military authorities; Economic Cooperation Administration; Foreign economic aid; Mission for Economic Cooperation

Apprentice training, 45

Arbeiterkammer Jahrbuch, *cited,* 20n, 26n, 29n, 33n, 50n, 52n

Arbeiter-Zeitung, *cited,* 16n, 26n, 28n-30n, 33n-35n, 39n, 44n, 47n-50n, 52n, 55n

Association of Austrian Industrialists, 29, 56

Austria, description of, 11; political institutions, 11, 14; *see specific organs*

Austrian Institute of Economic Research, 20, 23-24, 26, 29, 32, 34, 37, 43, 55; *see also* Institut für Wirtschaftsforschung

Austrian national bank, president of, 48

Bauer, Otto, 17

Black market prices, 20, 23, 29, 30, 31, 32, 36, 40, 71 Table; *see also* Cost and standard of living

Böhm, Karl, 44, 45, 49

Bonuses, 32, 37

Businessmen's interests, 11, 47, 67; *see also* Association of Austrian Industrialists; Chamber of Trade; People's party

Cabinet, 11, 28, 42

Central Wage Commission, 20, 21, 23

Chamber of Agriculture, 12-14, 28, 32-33, 36, 48, 54, 56, 58, 60, 62, 65, 68; functions of, 13; methods of, 63; *see also* Agricultural interests; Farmers

Chamber of Labor, 12-14, 16, 25, 28, 36, 43, 48, 50-52, 56, 60, 62, 65, 68; membership of, 13; voting procedure of, 13; functions of, 13, 16, 63; *see also* Labor interests

Chamber of Trade, 12, 14-15, 28-29, 33, 35-36, 41-44, 48, 51, 53, 56, 60, 62-63; conventions of, 14; functions of, 13, 63; membership of, 12; objectives, 41; officials, 12, 28, 30, 39; voting procedure of, 13; *see also* Businessmen's interests

Chancellor, 11, 48, 53

Children's allowances, *see* Family allowances

Collective bargaining, 9, 13-14, 24, 40, 46-47, 49, 51, 64-65; procedure, 16

Collective labor agreements, *see* Collective bargaining; Wage-price agreements

Communist party, 11, 15-16, 28, 35, 39, 43-45, 52-53, 56, 66

Constituent powers, 66; veto power of, 68

Cost and standard of living, 15, 18 Chart, 21, 23, 26, 28, 30, 34, 36-38, 46, 50, 52, 54-55, 57-58, 60, 67; *see also* Black market prices; Voluntary price cuts

Cost of living index, 20, 26-27, 29-30, 32, 34, 36, 40, 42, 46, 56, 70 Table; compilation of, 23, 33; *see also* Austrian Institute of Economic Research; Black market prices; Cost and standard of living

Coup d'état (attempted), *see* General strikes

Credit, 57, 64, 65, 67

Czechoslovakia, 50

Das Klein Volksblatt, *cited,* 25n-26n, 28n, 30n, 32n, 34n-35n, 39n, 51n

Denkschrift der Vereinigung Österreichischer Industrieller zur Währungsfrage, *cited,* 30n

Deutsch, Julius, 17

75